# PRAISE FOR
## TO UNSTOPPABLE

"We've all been 'stuck' before in our lives and our work—whether due to a traumatic event, burnout from the everyday grind, or just a general lack of confidence. Trish has provided an actionable playbook for building an unstoppable mindset and breaking through to a better you."

**—CLAIRE SHIPMAN,** four-time *New York Times* bestselling co-author of *The Confidence Code* and *Womenomics*

"Trish is the real deal—a superstar executive and leader. Whether you're trying to create a healthy and positive corporate culture, develop unbreakable resilience, or jump-start your team after a tough loss, this book is the perfect manual not only for getting back on track but for reaching new heights."

**—JOSH LINKNER,** five-time tech entrepreneur, venture capital investor, and *New York Times* bestselling author of *Disciplined Dreaming* and *Big Little Breakthroughs*

"The words and stories in this book are massive inspiration for anyone interested in taking their personal or professional life to the next level. Whether you're attempting to compose beautiful music, start a business, or just trying to get your life on track, at some point in your journey it's inevitable that you will get stuck. Trish's enlightening book provides all the tools needed to help you discover and refine that rhythm of greatness and spirit within yourself to get unstuck!"

**—NATHAN EAST,** Grammy-nominated recording artist, bassist, producer, educator, and keynote speaker

"Just as I've experienced firsthand with Trish herself, her book inspires and encourages from start to finish. The moment that you start reading *From Stuck to Unstoppable*, you will be motivated to take the steps forward to become 'unstuck' in your own life and pass on those tools to those around you. This book is the perfect reminder that even though we don't get to choose what happens to us, we get to choose how we react and we get to find beauty in the process of becoming unstoppable."

**—SYDNEY SIEROTA,** founder and lead singer of the multiplatinum-selling band Echosmith, and cowriter of the wildly popular hit song "Cool Kids"

"Every executive is trying to get themselves and their company to the next level. Trish's book is a practical, reflective guide to gaining awareness of the ways individuals and teams can get stuck—whether from a traumatic event or from the inertia of daily life—and provides actionable steps to unleashing profound personal and professional growth."

**—CAROL SEYMOUR,** CEO/founder of Signature Leaders and author of *Wisdom Warriors*

"*From Stuck to Unstoppable* is a profoundly inspirational handbook chock-full of practical advice for working, leading, and living with passion and purpose. Trish's common-sense authenticity and moving personal story will inspire you to set aside the excuses and become unstoppable!"

**—CHARLENE WHEELESS,** author of *You Are Enough!*, TEDx speaker, and MG100 leadership coach

"*From Stuck to Unstoppable* is a powerful reminder that—whether it's a minor setback or a major catastrophe—we can all choose to become unstuck. Trish's inspiring story and decades of hard-earned wisdom as a corporate leader provide a must-read playbook for becoming your best, unstoppable self!"

**—VAL RIES,** author of *Chief Inspiration Officer* and founder of Executive Muse

"I absolutely love the concept Trish has mastered! As we all go through moments in our life when we feel stuck, it can be very difficult to pivot. But Trish gives us the blueprint not just to pivot but to conquer the stuck feeling and become UNSTOPPABLE! She lives and breathes it, and it shows in her majestic writing!"

—**DAVID NURSE,** NBA life optimization coach, keynote speaker, and bestselling author of *Pivot & Go*

amplifypublishinggroup.com

*From Stuck to Unstoppable: The Power of Intentional Decision-Making in Life and Leadership*

**For more information, please contact:**
An imprint of Amplify Publishing Group
620 Herndon Parkway, Suite 320
Herndon, VA 20170
info@amplifypublishing.com

Library of Congress Control Number: 2022911784

CPSIA Code: PRV0123A

ISBN-13: 978-1-63755-411-1

Printed in the United States

*To all the setbacks and tragedies
and all the comebacks and triumphs,
for which I am extremely grateful.*

# FROM STUCK TO
# UNSTOPPABLE

*The Power of Intentional Decision-Making
in Life and Leadership*

# TRISH HUNT

an imprint of Amplify Publishing Group

# CONTENTS

# Foreword

IF YOU HAVE EVER UNDERESTIMATED what you can achieve or felt like giving up because you'd stopped moving forward in your life or career, read this book.

I have known Trish Hunt for thirty years, first meeting her at Walt Disney World in 1992 when she was a young management trainee. She was also one of the first Disney Partners in Excellence winners—an award which is given to a very small percentage of cast members for excellence in performance.

Trish—like many of us—has experienced serious obstacles in her life, but they have not stopped her commitment to excellence with her loved ones or in her career. Her rise from a young Disney World front line cast member to her current role as division president of consumer health at a S&P 500 company, with executive roles along the way in banking, shows the formula that leads to success.

You may be stuck in the wrong town, the wrong relationship, or the wrong career. You may suffer from poor health, poor education, or bad finances. You may have the wrong attitude or the wrong boss, or you may be at the wrong company . . . the list of wrongs could be a mile long.

In this book, Trish reminds us of the important truth that we are not a product of our circumstances but are a product of our decisions.

Chapter Six, for example, focuses on the timeless advice that there are "No Silver Platters." A lot of people subscribe to the theory that all you need is a good education—but I can tell you from many painful experiences that it's just not true.

Like Trish I encountered many obstacles in my life, from being fired to being passed over for a promotion—which I thought was wrong—to having to care for my wife, Priscilla, for two years when she almost died from a failed surgery. Education did not help me get through those times.

What resolved each of those obstacles was my positive attitude and reputation for being a can-do, get-it-done, never-quit leader. No matter what job I ever had, from potato peeler and cook in the Army to the best, most reliable, most competent waiter at Hilton to a vice president at Marriott to the head of Disney World operations, it was my hard work, reliability, ability to learn on the job, and respect for everybody that were responsible for my success. The only silver platters were the ones I served the food from.

I'm also a big fan of another concept that Trish talks about—the Power of Pause, which can help you reassess your situation and get refocused on a new path. There are many forks in the roads in all parts of our lives. Most people go down the wrong fork way too far, sometimes because it is comfortable and provides them with a sense of security but not a great life.

For several years, I found myself going down the wrong path as an effective, get-it-done, take-no-prisoners manager. I accomplished a lot but left a lot of emotionally wounded associates along the way.

I received a wake-up call when one of my managers admitted to me that he was terrified of me visiting his hotel. He'd even had to be transported to the hospital for observation the day I arrived. We had dinner together that night, and he admitted to me that he was terribly intimidated and downright afraid of me from my reputation.

After that experience, I took a pause to understand myself and to understand what I needed to do to be a good manager and a great leader. That transition took time. I became aware that the faults in my style sprang from my own insecurities and fear of failure. The pause helped me to backtrack down that fork in the road and to take the other fork. I was stuck as an autocratic manager and eventually became an unstoppable leader.

The bottom line is that being in the wrong situation may or may not be your fault—but staying in it is your fault. You will learn that making the right decisions to get UNSTUCK is hard. But if you don't make the hard decisions, life becomes even harder.

Trish's story is proof that staying stuck is a choice, and it is never too late to get UNSTUCK and then become UNSTOPPABLE.

**—Lee Cockerell,**
executive vice president, Walt Disney World® Resort (retired and inspired), and author of six books on leadership, management, culture, career, and customer service, including *Creating Magic* and *The Customer Rules*

"What a precious privilege it is to be alive—to breathe, to think, to enjoy, to love."

—Marcus Aurelius

*Introduction*

# THE POWER OF CONSTANT, CONSCIOUS CHOICE

I AM DEEPLY GRATEFUL that you have chosen to join me on this journey. The gratitude that I feel is real; it runs deep within me, like the current of a river. It's important for me to express this gratitude right at the outset; it needs to be our first order of business. I am glad that you're here.

*Welcome.*

And now, I must ask a small favor: Before we even take our first step forward, I ask that you take a quick step back. Go back, for a moment, to my very first sentence. There are two words within that sentence that are essential. These two words will ground and guide us as we move forward—and taken together, they capture the essence and the spirit of the book in its entirety. So let's swing back to the beginning, since the beginning is always a great place to start.

Read those first words again. Slowly. Carefully. Let the words in that sentence sink down deep. I'll give it to you again:

*I am deeply grateful that you have chosen to join me on this journey.*

The first operative word?

*Chosen.*

This is a book that recognizes and celebrates our ability to make conscious choices. That you have *chosen* to join me, to walk with me, and to examine and explore this notion of choice is both important and thematically significant.

What we will learn, as we move through the chapters of this book, is that the power of choice belongs to each and every one of us. It belongs to me. It belongs to you. It belongs to all of us. And while we certainly move through life facing our own, singularly unique set of circumstances—the challenges I face are different than the challenges you face, because we are different people leading different lives—what draws us together into a common human embrace is the fact that we all carry within us the beautifully innate ability *to choose.*

But this is more than an innate ability. It is also an extraordinary gift. The power to choose how we move through life—when crisis strikes, for instance, will we remain mentally paralyzed or will we propel ourselves forward?—is a precious gift that belongs to each of us.

Here's the bottom line: the gift of conscious choice gives us *options.* We can either stay stuck within the messy confines of our own discomfort, we can "press pause" for a moment and stand still before regrouping, or we can push ourselves through. Stay stuck, press pause, or push through. The most important thing to remember is that whatever we decide to do, however we decide to react, whichever options we decide to exercise, the choice belongs to us.

No, we cannot control all of the external events that unfold around us as we live our lives, but we *can* control our ability to respond and react to those events. And it is within these precious, powerful moments of choice where growth usually lives. Where transformation lives. Where happiness, dignity, compassion, and grace live.

Sadly, though, many of us seem to have forgotten that this gift belongs to us. We have conditioned ourselves, either consciously or unconsciously, to plod through life unaware that the power of choice is ours. We forget that the power of choice *lives within us.* We forget that there is another way to respond to crisis and chaos, another way to manage missteps and setbacks. We forget that we can choose forward-moving propulsion rather than fear-based paralysis! That we can choose faith over fear. Action over inaction. We forget.

This book will help us remember.

We can *choose* to become unstuck. We can *choose* to place ourselves on a trajectory that moves us from stuck to unstoppable . . . if we make the conscious, purposeful decision to do so, that is. No, the process won't always be smooth and it won't always be easy, but it will always be an option available to us, so we must decide to exercise that option!

This will require a reset of our mental mindset. It will require that we train—and *re*train—our brains so that we become vitally aware of the fact that this thing called choice is always ours, even when life gets messy and sloppy and unpredictable and painful. (In fact, our moments of "being stuck" don't always have to be dripping in over-the-top drama. Even everyday moments of paralysis—"I don't have the energy or desire to get off out of bed today!"—can be just as debilitating as the Dramatically Debilitating Moments like losing a job or facing the sudden death of a loved one. When it comes to crisis, *everything counts*, from the minor missteps to the over-the-cliff catastrophes. It doesn't take a monumental setback to push us into the stuck position; the minor "ankle-biters" can be just as debilitating. The long and short of it is that, well, *stuck is stuck*.)

Bottom line: this book will give you the tools you need to move through these challenging moments—no matter their degree of intensity—in a way that allows you to find the other side. The good news is that there is another side. You can get to the other side of a bad moment if you make the conscious decision to do it. Getting there can be tricky, though. It's hard to push through when what you really want to do is stay still, or suffer through your setback slowly and take your time licking your wounds. It's difficult to choose movement over paralysis . . . but it can be done, because the choice, again, is ours. This journey we're taking together is all about the beauty of choice.

So I thank you for making the conscious choice to pick this book up and begin this journey with me. The very fact that you are holding it in your hands at this moment is a ringing affirmation that you *do* recognize the power of choice. And that you have chosen to walk with me, to read my words, to explore these practices and principles is, to me, a blessing of untold magnitude. I am hopeful that the lessons in this book will expand your perspective and widen your vision. More than hopeful, I am *confident*. I am confident that this book will set you on a new and unstoppable path.

I want us to swing back to the beginning yet again. Let's return to that very first sentence of this Introduction and examine the second operative word. We already know the first word was "chosen." The second word is equally powerful, and I chose it, too, with purpose and intention.

That word: *journey.*

What we are about to embark upon is a journey indeed. In fact, I'd describe it as a two-part journey: a literary journey and a life journey as well.

The literary journey will involve our traveling together through the orderly, sequential pages of the book itself. But on a far more expansive level, we will also travel through the multi-layered, ongoing journey of life itself, exploring and discovering how we can navigate this constantly unfolding process of living in a way that allows us to push ahead with purpose and power.

One journey—the literary journey—is finite; it will end when you come to the last page. But the other journey—the journey from stuck to unstoppable—is infinite. Constant. Ever-evolving. This is the journey that will begin after the book is finished— because after the book is finished, you will be outfitted with the tools you need to live life fully, without fear of failure. To live and to lead others from a place of balance, equilibrium, and clarity.

Both journeys are vital. And like any journey, we cannot begin either without taking that first important single step . . . which we have already taken together. From here, the only place to move, the best place to move, the *perfect* place to move, is forward. We will move forward together.

———

I want to reflect, for a moment, on what has driven me to write this book. This is important simply because it leads me to this singular, stunning revelation: over the course of my personal and professional life—more than five decades of living, three decades as a corporate leader, and four decades spent enduring and embracing intense change (which I will delve into later)—it is far more accurate to say that this book has been writing itself.

By virtue of living my life, by experiencing all that I've experienced, and by encountering all that I have encountered, I am now ready, able, and *equipped* to share some of the lessons I've learned in a way that I hope will be relevant and applicable to you in your own life.

To say it another way, if I hadn't encountered all the setbacks, all the victories, all the joys, all the trajectories and, yes, even all the tragedies—all the *everything* that makes up this human life of mine—this book would simply not be.

For my entire life, then, this book has been writing itself: an experience would unfold in my life—major or minor, negative or positive—and within that moment would be a golden nugget of experiential wisdom. What would unfold with that moment would be a bit of new insight or perhaps even an "aha!" moment of inspired reflection.

These are the lessons and the lived experiences I will share with you. Thirty years ago, for instance, I could not have written this book. It was not my book to write. I was not the same person I am today. I hadn't yet experienced all that I was meant to experience; hadn't encountered all that I was meant to encounter. It might even be accurate to say that I hadn't stayed stuck long enough to have written a book about the joy and freedom that comes from becoming *unstuck*. So in a very real way, the passage of time and the accumulation of life experiences are what have equipped me to write this book and share these lived experiences.

Knowing what it *feels like* to be stuck, and what it *looks like* to be stuck is what has allowed me to pick up my pen and write this book. I am, by nature, a person who is deeply steeped in what I will call a "common sense sensibility." Though I will delve into this more deeply in the first chapter, this is how my mother raised me: to find solutions, to find a way out, to find a way around, to find a way through.

I am practical, no-nonsense, and relentlessly solution-driven—yet even so, I have experienced tumultuous, life-altering moments because I am something else, too: I am *human*. I am flawed. I am vulnerable. I might not spend a lot of time *staying* stuck, but I've suffered through major (and minor) crises that have changed the course of my life as a leader, as a woman, a mother, a sister, a friend, and a human being. I write this book to share the life lessons and enduring principles that have evolved from these experiences.

There is nothing more important to me than sharing these principles, because I believe they are life-changing, life-defining, and even life-*saving*. Whether you're a corporate executive, an entrepreneur, or a parent—even if you're not in the leadership world at all but are simply trying to live your daily life with greater care and a more powerful sense of purpose—I write this book to show you how to propel past the painful, sticky, messy points you're inevitably going to encounter.

I write the words because I have already lived the experiences. Yes, messiness, discord, and imbalance will invariably unfold as we live our lives—this is the nature of the human condition, is it not?—but the coping tools and techniques I have developed over the years will help to push you through. These tools have opened doors to me that I once thought had been slammed shut forever. I write this book to open those doors for you, too, and to remind you that those doors—the doors that lead to growth, to happiness, to professional success, to emotional balance, to mental clarity, and to emotional equilibrium—do indeed still exist, even if they feel like they've been slammed shut.

I write this book to remind you that there are blocked entrances in your life that are waiting to swing open; there are windows and rooftops, trap doors, and secret passageways that are waiting to be discovered and flung open so that you can step through. I write this book to remind you that, even if you might feel stuck, there are tools and techniques, practices and principles, that will move you from stuck to unstoppable.

You just have to keep searching for these openings. You must find those locked windows and closed doors, fling them wide open, and step through and stand, tall and proud, in the wide-open spaces of your own authentic truth. You can push your way past stuck.

---

A brief word about the structure and arrangement of the book itself. Although we will explore, in each chapter, a different aspect of how best to push ourselves along this powerful trajectory from stuck to unstoppable, there will not be a strict sequence or an iron-clad chronology we must follow that dictates how this trajectory unfolds.

We will start with important foundational concepts, of course, then we'll do a deeper dive into these concepts as we move into each successive chapter. The sequence should feel comfortable, fully integrated, and pleasingly holistic.

Essentially, the book will be presented in a way that allows you to "cherry-pick" your way through the concepts and explore the principles that resonate most deeply with you. My promise to you is this: wherever you are on your journey, *I will meet you there.*

In terms of arrangement, you'll also see a single, common thread woven into the fabric of many of the chapters—a story to which I will continually refer in every chapter that we'll use as a "pivot point" for further discussion and deeper exploration.

Let me explain. My mission and goal is to teach and illuminate you in a way that will allow you to move your organization, your employees, or perhaps just your general mindset as a human being trying to live your life, from a place of being stuck to a place of being unstoppable. I am in the business of creating this trajectory for other people. To me, there is nothing more important.

As a way to reach my audiences, whether it's a live audience or a reading audience, I like to draw from the depth and breadth of my own human experience. But some time ago, someone whom I deeply admire and respect also urged me to draw on the stories and experiences of *other humans* to help bring these decidedly human points home. He urged me to become "a collector of stories" and to share the human stories of others in a way that helps illuminate and expand my own themes and principles.

The rationale certainly makes sense. By drawing from the deep well of others' experiences, we learn from them in a way that feels authentic and complete. When we listen to others' voices, when we learn from their lived experiences, we expand our knowledge base exponentially. For this very reason, I will be turning to other voices to help shine light onto how best we can move from stuck to unstoppable. My own voice will obviously be important in this book . . . but it is not be the *only* voice you will hear. You will hear others. This is how we grow, discover, and learn. Because I am a collector of voices, these voices will ring loud and clear in each chapter.

Here's what I mean: Throughout the book, I will reference the story of two inspirational women, Trina Spear and Heather Hasson, whose stuck-to-unstoppable trajectory will help frame various points of discussion. Trina and Heather, beautifully ordinary women who took extraordinary steps to push past their "stuck points," will serve as the pivot point for deeper discussion of the various principles we'll explore. My focus on them will be brief, but they offer a useful thematic touchstone for our journey towards self-discovery.

A bit of background: Trina Spear and Heather Hasson, both registered nurses, ended up redefining, revolutionizing, and completely reimagining the health care apparel industry as we know it today. Singlehandedly—yet *together*—as a result of their hard work, their dogged determination, and their refusal to settle for anything less than the vision they had clearly laid out for themselves, they developed and designed medical scrubs that were comfortable, fashionable, and highly functional.

For years, Trina and Heather refined and perfected the

prototypes for these scrubs. They even sold them from the trunks of their cars! The point is that they were in alignment, at all times. Their collective vision, as well as their commitment to motivate and inspire each other, was clear. At the time the company went public on the New York Stock Exchange, it was valued at more than $6 *billion* (yes, that's billion with a *B).* The company, called FIGS, is the perfect example of how a company (and within it, the individuals) can move from stuck to unstoppable.

This story serves as the perfect thematic touchpoint for a larger discussion about how we push past fear, doubt, and anxiety to arrive at a more productive place. I will use their amazing journey similarly within the pages of this book. We can *all* be fired up by the FIGS story; we can all be inspired and energized by the flame of fierce determination these two women generated between them a flame that ended up redefining an entire industry.

Throughout my life and especially over the course of my thirty years of corporate experience, I have talked with lots of people; I've heard lots of vital, visionary voices. I hear them because I listen to them—and I listen to them because I *seek them out*. I choose to listen, and because I listen closely, I learn.

Throughout my career, I have been fortunate enough to have traveled around the globe—more than two million miles. During that time, I sought out the voices of those who would speak to me about human resilience. Over the course of my world travels, I've spoken with scores of people who have suffered unthinkable tragedy and who have sustained unimaginable setbacks. I've spoken with people who must live with profound disabilities . . . but who have managed to move beyond their disabilities to a place of acceptance, grace, and extraordinary mental resilience. I've heard stories on human trafficking, spoken to people who escaped Nazi Germany, heard from people who have suffered unimaginable horror and strife . . . but who have refused to stay stuck. These are people who have lost it all, then built it back with dignity and pride.

We can all hold within us this same sort of resilience and grit—no matter what challenges or circumstances we face. It is there, waiting for us to tap into it. Individually and collectively, it belongs to us. We must learn to rely on one another for this sense of collective resilience; to learn from one another's unique stories and life experiences, because in a very real sense, we all *belong to* each other!

We are a collection—a chorus!—of voices.

This is too joyous a song to sing alone.

———

A final word: Throughout my life, I have always been drawn, somehow, to the art of interior design. I know this sounds a bit off-topic, but humor me here for a moment, because I'm certain that my rationale will eventually resonate in a way that makes sense.

Even as a child, I always had a deep, abiding passion for finding the beauty and order in my surroundings. As a single mother raising three children, my mother didn't have much at all—but what she did have, she managed to make beautiful.

My mother made our surroundings comfortable, aesthetically pleasing, and most important of all, she made them feel *safe*. We didn't have much . . . but we had everything we needed, thanks to my mother's determined spirit. She gave us a home filled with pride.

In many ways, I want this book to feel like a home to you. In each chapter, we will explore a different room. We will enter each room with a sense of purpose and intention, searching for wisdom and looking for lessons that will enlighten us. We will enter each room, move through each chapter, as if we were moving through a beautiful, previously unexplored new home. As we enter, we'll unlock each door, throw back the curtains, and fling open every window. This is a book about designing and building your best life, your best "home."

In my own home today, there is nothing more joyful and stabilizing than hunkering down in my sunlit library with an open journal and a cup of hot tea. Or sitting around the big farm table in the kitchen, surrounded by the warmth, laughter, and love of my own family. Every room in my home counts—just as *every day in my life counts*. I like to live purposefully and with great intention.

There are six empty shelves in my library. This is by design. I keep them empty as way to remind me that I don't have to keep them full! I want to be intentional and thoughtful about how I feel (and fill) the space around me; random knick-knacks and space-fillers are not necessary, nor are they healthy. I keep those six shelves open to remind me that there is always room and always space to grow. I must give myself the luxury of this conscious choice.

This is how I want you to feel about this book. I want it to be a safe space for you—a space where you can grow and thrive and reflect. In fact, I encourage you to leave some empty space within the "shelves" and the pages of this book so that you can reflect and record. I encourage you to write down your thoughts as you read; jot down your reactions to the concepts we explore. Let your pulse be felt within the pages of this book. Be a note-taker and journal-keeper. This is certainly how I live. I want this book to reflect the way I live my own life . . . but more important, you need to customize the principles within this book so that they reflect the way you live and lead yours!

So open these pages now, and let's step into the first chapter. Together, let's move from room to room, chapter to chapter. By the time we are finished with the finite journey that is this book, you will be prepared to launch a new journey towards continued self-discovery and expansion that is infinite and ongoing.

Two journeys. Both vital.
Come join me. Take my outstretched hand.
Step with me into this first room.
Let's let the journey begin.

## *Chapter One*
# MY STORY

"There's been an accident."

Since we want each chapter of this book to feel like a comfortable room within the literary home we are building, let's swing open this first door and step inside.

I'm glad you're with me on this particular journey, because this is not an easy door to swing open; it opens onto one of the most traumatic-yet-transformative periods of my entire life. Without a doubt, it is fitting and appropriate to begin my "story" with this event, simply because the moment itself (and everything that unfolded afterward as a result) has informed and influenced the kind of leader and the kind of human I am today.

We *all* have defining, life-altering moments, the kind of moments that mark our lives and hold within them the potential to either bend us or break us. The kind of moments that either kill us or make us stronger.

If I had been anyone else but the no-nonsense, practical, problem-solving, push-through-it person I was raised to be, I doubt that I would be here today, writing this book and sharing these concepts. I might not have survived. But the indisputable fact of the matter is that I *did*—and the very reason I survived then is the same reason I thrive today: because staying stuck is not a viable option for me.

As we step into this first room—my bright, new, sun-splashed bedroom in Phoenix, Arizona—what we'll experience first is sound rather than sight, the sound of four words that changed my life forever. If I listen closely enough, I can still hear those words today, clear as a bell, tumbling like heavy stones from the stranger's voice on the other end of the phone:

"There's been an accident."

Because my body was already going into shock, the words I heard next were muffled and indistinct . . . yet, strange as it may sound, each word also sounded alarmingly clear, as sharp and precise as a surgeon's scalpel. Things were coming undone. Moving too fast. My body began to shake. Breathing became difficult. Through that awful moment, though, I still held the phone to my ear, listening:

". . . get here quickly . . ."

I remember slipping down to the side of the bed as she spoke. The shaking was harder now, the lump in my throat brought hot tears. What was this person *saying* to me? This couldn't be real. A loving husband, two beautiful little children, a new job—our four wonderful lives stretched out before us, waiting to be lived.

But the voice on the other end of the phone kept talking. It was the phone call that every spouse or partner, every mother or father, absolutely dreads. In my sunny bedroom in Phoenix, the velocity of the words coming at me had knocked me, quite literally, to the floor.

I still listened, though. Even from my sitting/crouching

position on the side of the bed, I still held that phone to my ear. Yes, the words I was hearing were horrible words to hear, but I listened to them because *not* listening was not an option. For the sake and the safety of my two small children, I had to hear what was being said to me in that moment. Staying stuck—even in my shock and anguish—was simply not a choice I could make. I needed to push myself through. I needed to force myself to deal with the matter at hand. Lives were at stake.

"... serious car accident ..."

"... take the next flight out ..."

Within minutes, after calling an aunt who also lived in Phoenix to come stay with my children, I was racing to the airport. Racing towards my husband in Orlando, who'd just sustained grave injuries in a car accident. Racing towards a life that would soon be upended and rearranged in ways that I could never have imagined.

I'd just relocated to Phoenix to take an exciting new job; we'd barely unpacked the bags and boxes. I'd just left my job as a professional at Disney, walking away from all of my trusted colleagues, all of my friends, and everything that was important and familiar to me. Day one of my new job hadn't even come. My husband, Howie, hadn't even joined us yet ... not yet ... not yet.

It's ironic, isn't it, how the "not-yets" in our lives often never have a chance to fully materialize because sudden, unexpected circumstances swoop in and snatch them away? If nothing else, the lesson we can take from these unexpected twists and turns is the awareness that while we might not be able to control how and when these unexpected moments arrive, we *can* control our reaction to them once they do. Even in the worst moments, we have the ability and inner capacity to push through and persevere. No, that doesn't stop the pain or ease the shock or change the final outcome of the crisis we're up against, but it does give us a measure of control and solidity. And when you're standing in the midst of crisis and/or uncertainty, knowing you have a measure of self-control can mean the difference between being stuck and getting *un*stuck.

I landed in Orlando several hours later and headed straight to the hospital. My family and close friends met me there. They surrounded me and remained around me at every moment. My mother, of course, never left my side. She was (and is) my rock and my foundation. Even today, she pushes and propels me past the tough spots. Isn't this what we must do for each other, as humans?

I need to digress here for a moment, because there is both a leadership and a life lesson here as well: during times of crisis—whether it's a crisis within your organization or a personal crisis in your daily life—we must learn to rely on the trusted people around us to help us navigate through. Senior executives and leaders at all levels often forget this. We operate so often under the mistaken assumption that we are invincible, that we are self-sufficient and self-driven and should therefore be dependent upon no one but ourselves, that we miss the opportunity to seek the guidance, the support, and, yes, sometimes even the comfort of our colleagues and cohorts.

Creating an organizational culture of trust, transparency, and openness is vital, not just for us, but for the team members and employees we lead. And it is this kind of culture—a culture that believes in supporting, enabling, and empowering one another, particularly when challenges arise—that enables everyone, at every level, to work towards becoming consistently unstoppable. This not only makes good business sense. *It just makes good sense.* In all of your dealings, then, try to ensure that you create a culture that is caring and compassionate. It makes a difference.

It certainly made a difference to me that day, being surrounded by people who cared. Suddenly, at the hospital, I found myself stepping into yet another room that would alter the course of my life forever: the intensive care unit. Yet another room that would bring unexpected change, immeasurable grief, and a seismic shift in my life circumstance.

I pushed open the door.

There lay my Howie, so small in his hospital bed, surrounded by buzzing, beeping machines and whooshing tubes that were keeping him alive. For the next three days, I sat with him. Lay beside him. Stroked his face. Consulted with doctors. Felt the comforting presence of my close friends and family. For three days, I prayed over him, with him, and for him.

At ten in the morning on the fourth day, with the sun streaming into his room and my head resting gently on his stomach, my arms wrapped gently around his legs, Howie took his last breath.

It was his twenty-ninth birthday.

——————

## The Power of the Pause

Flying back to Phoenix to tell my children that they would now have to grow up in a world without their father was one of the most difficult things I've ever had to do. But here's the thing: *I did it*. I did it because I had to. I did it because, just as I'd mentioned earlier, *not* doing it was simply not an option. I was now a grieving new widow—but on a far more visceral, far more practical, even a far more *primitive* level, I was also, suddenly, the fiercely protective mother of my two small (and now fatherless) children who needed me to be fully present for them.

Of course, I was dealing with the shock, the grief, and the sharp pain of losing my beloved, but still, in the back of my mind, the more practical decisions I knew I was going to have to make very, very soon were already forming into actionable strategies. By that, I mean this: as bad as the situation was, I knew I had to take immediate steps to deal with it for the sake of my two innocent children.

I had a choice to make—the biggest choice of my life: I could choose to let this tragedy define my life and my children's lives, where we would live our years in anger, pain, and regret . . . or I could push through the pain to stand strong for my children, to survive for my own sake, and to work towards the goal of not just surviving, but *thriving* again, one day.

Still, the questions swirled: Was I going to crumble? How would I put bread on the table? How would I find the strength to walk into my office on the first day of my new job? When would this pain end? Would I be able to protect, provide for, and nurture my two children in the way that they needed and deserved?

I already knew the answer to that last question, about protecting and providing for my kids, before I even asked it. The answer was that I *must* protect them. My love for my children and my instinctive desire to protect and provide for them was deeper even than my grief. But how would I make it from one moment to the next without the one other person in the world with the same vested interest in them as me?

Looking back on it now, I realize that I already knew the answers to *all* of these questions, even as I was asking them. I knew that I had to push forward, to move past stuck, to propel past my pain . . . but I still had to allow myself the luxury of sitting in my brokenness for a moment. I still had to allow myself the sensation of knowing what it feels like and what it looks like to stand still, for a minute, in the midst of my grief.

This is important for all of us.
It is perfectly acceptable to take a
momentary "pause" in the midst of your
crisis—just be sure the pause that you
take is just that: momentary.

In our rush towards success, towards continued ascension in the corporate ranks, or to whatever victory we hope to achieve next in our professional or personal lives, we should always try to remember the power that is held within that all-important pause. That pause is what often gives us the perspective we need to plot our next steps and push through our crisis with renewed strength.

For those first several weeks after my husband's death, in those heavy, grief-filled days after we said goodbye to him forever and I flew back to Phoenix, I took that pause. I put my kids in daycare, which helped establish a sense of normalcy and routine in their own little lives. I called my boss and told him I'd need a little while longer before I started my new position. I turned inward. I isolated. I reflected. I stood in the center of what it felt like to be bent and heartbroken. I spent quiet, contemplative time with myself. I journaled. I hiked. I prayed. I prayed some more—and, yes, I *paused*. And eventually, it was within the quiet places of those pauses where I gradually found the strength I needed to keep pushing forward.

The lesson here is that we must take time to understand and absorb what it *feels like* to be stuck before we can take definitive steps towards becoming unstuck. Even as leaders, we are not automatons. We are not perfectly designed. No. We are flawed, we are human, and we must remind ourselves (and remind each other, as well as our team members and employees) that it is important to take time to contemplate, to reflect, and even to stand in the stillness of being stuck, at least momentarily.

We all have moments and days when we feel anxious. Overloaded. Isolated. On edge. Set apart. Afraid. Let's learn to honor those feelings—they are real, after all!—without letting them paralyze us. Let's also take the time to figure out where these feelings are coming from, to discover their root source. This requires a purposeful pause. But after we take that pause, we move forward. That is what this book is all about: moving forward to become the architects, the artists, and the sculptors of our own masterpieces, of our own outcomes. The choice is totally and completely up to us.

*You* get to choose to be positive instead of negative, to go left instead of right, to become the victor instead of the victim, to move from a place of fear to a place of faith. That choice is always yours.

Forgive the repetition, but I am moved to write these words again, simply because they are so important:

The choice is always yours.

———————

## The Kid Who Was Consistently Unstoppable

As a child, I frequently found myself pushing my little life from stuck to unstoppable. Don't misunderstand. I didn't raise myself, but my mom was busy. She didn't have time for any nonsense, and her expectations of my brothers and me were clear. My mother raised me and my two older brothers in a home filled with love and light. We might not have had much, but somehow we always had everything we needed. Granted, there were many years where she struggled to keep food on the table and clothes on our backs, but she constantly rose to the task, and she constantly infused happiness into our home and into our hearts.

In fact, my mother was the first person who showed me, up close and personal, what "unstoppable" really *looked* like. She's the one who created the "unstoppable" mold in my young life—a mold that still fits my life today. And much later in life, as fate would have it, she was the person who helped ease me into the sudden, shocking role of single motherhood. She raised three children as a single mother and I would one day come to raise my own children as a single mother. These early life lessons and mother-daughter parallels are what helped propel me forward.

Looking back on it, I realize my mother was an artist—an artist of life and living. Even as a child, she painted the portrait of "unstoppable" for me in colors that were clear and vivid and wildly wonderful. In fact, she *was* the brush . . . and our lives were the canvas.

I was ten years old when my parents divorced, and with the divorce, the colors on our "life canvas" changed drastically. More than anything, our financial situation became a bit darker and bleaker. This brought all kinds of challenges, some small, some not-so-small.

Shortly after the divorce, my mom told me that she could no longer afford my dance lessons. Even today, in the space of this very moment as I am writing these words, the shock and disappointment come flooding back. No more dance lessons? How could this *be*? My dance lessons brought me so much joy—not just the joy of the movement itself and the joy of socializing with my girlfriends, but the joy that came from performing and from perfecting a particular position and mastering a certain step until I'd gotten it "just right." Now, suddenly, all of those "just right" moments were being taken away from me.

You're probably getting to know me a bit better as we continue our literary journey together, so it might not surprise you to hear how I handled the No More Dance Lessons bombshell. You guessed it: I pushed past it. I created a solution. Even at the young age of ten, I was already wired to be a solution-finder. I went directly to my dance teacher, Mrs. Marks, and apprised her of the situation—and I did it without preamble, without fear, and without apology. I told the remarkable Mrs. Marks that my family and I were no longer in the position to pay for the classes. And then I proposed a creative solution: Would she consider letting me teach one of the younger dance classes in exchange for free classes?

Her immediate response: "Certainly!"

> The lesson here is that if you are served a setback, don't let it knock you permanently off-course. Get resourceful.

Dig down deep and find your grit. Keep pushing forward. Be brave, unapologetic, and radically creative as you develop viable alternatives. If you don't do this for yourself, no one else will, so always find a way to evolve into the very best version of yourself that you possibly can be, even—perhaps *especially*—in the most challenging situations.

As I moved from elementary school to high school, our financial straits, unfortunately, persisted. When I was a senior in high school, I was voted both homecoming queen and president of my class. I could pretty much perform the executive duties of my leadership role as class president without any obvious or sustaining financial setbacks or sacrifices . . . but homecoming queen was a horse of a different color.

As homecoming queen, I was asked to represent our high school in a state-wide pageant—a pretty big deal by any standard, and bigger still given that we lived in the state of New York. Competition would be fierce. Talented, brilliant, beautiful young ladies from all over the state would be entering.

It was my mother—my hero, my anchor, and the rudder of my ship—who steered me towards a solution. Mom told me to march right down to our local JCPenney and speak directly with the manager, explain the situation, and ask for help.

Another important side note here: You probably have a similar "anchor" and "rudder" in your own life, too—the person who steers you back when you veer off-course and holds you steady when the wind threatens to untether you from your goals, your dreams, and your hopes. If you didn't have that certain someone (or a bunch of certain *someones*) in your life as you rose in position and power, you would be not where you are today. We all have them. When it comes right down to it, we really are an interconnected web of human beings who depend upon each other for protection, advancement, and growth.

Anyway, if someone like this still exists in your life, *stop what you're doing right now*—even if it means putting this book put down for a moment—to reach out and thank them for their presence. Call them up. Write them a note. Dash off an email. Text them. However you do it, *just do it*. We need to take the time from our busy, self-directed lives to express gratitude to those who have stood by us and stood up for us when we needed it most. Whether it's a corporate mentor or, in my case, a courageous mom, stop what you're doing for a second to perform a spontaneous act of gratitude.

That's what I'm going to do. I'm going to send a shout-out to my own mother, right here and right now, to express my gratitude for her grit, her grace, and her constant presence in my life. So I write three simple words right here in the pages of my book, and as I write them, I'm also saying them out loud: "Thank you, Mom."

But back to the pageant. Back to the "money-is-tight" issues that were standing in my way. What did I do? I followed my mom's direction, I put one foot in front of the other (as is my way), and I walked myself straight down to the JCPenney (not exactly a hop, skip, and a jump, but a two- or three-mile trek), and—just as I'd done with Mrs. Marks and my dance classes—I threw my cards on the table. I remember it like it was yesterday: this teenage version of myself striding into the store, asking for the manager, biting back my fear, choosing action over paralysis, and saying what I had to say.

I told the manager the situation, that I didn't have the resources to buy all the dresses, the gowns, and the fancy outfits that would be required for me to compete in the pageant, and then—as always—I offered up an option: Would the store consider *sponsoring* me in this pageant? And then, with grace and humility, I produced a list of all the things that I would need: the dresses and the gowns and the undergarments and the shoes—all of it.

Needless to say, the answer that came back was a resounding "yes."

My theory was and is that you can't get what you need unless you either ask for it or produce it yourself.

Those are the two options. It is a principle that was drilled into me even during my youth. This same drive, this same entrepreneurial spirit about life and leadership can be intentionally infused into each and every one of us.

For me, practicing this principle is innate; it is instinctive. It is what I and my two older brothers were raised to believe, and we saw not just the principle but the *practice* and the *mindset* made manifest in our own mother. She brought this stuff to life for us. She made it real.

We all have within us the capacity to develop and nurture this relentless entrepreneurial spirit—not just in ourselves but in the employees we lead, the loved ones we nurture and protect, and the people around us we inspire. In me, this entrepreneurial spirit is innate—it is woven into every strand of my DNA—but in other people it might have to be drawn out. Dusted off. Polished up. Buffed a bit. Brought to life.

My point is, whether you were trained to push through the challenges and setbacks in your life at an early age (like I was) or whether this is a newly acquired skill that you are just learning by virtue of opening this book and joining me on this journey, remember that *the option of tapping into this skill is available to us all.*

The path that will propel you past your own paralysis is within you, just waiting to be discovered. Granted, this path might be a little hard to find because you've used it so infrequently—it might be strewn with debris, covered with fallen branches, and hidden from plain sight—but I make this promise to you here and now: It is there. It exists. You just have to find it.

———————

Even my very earliest memories of being "consistently un-stoppable" remain bright and vivid on my life canvas today. Remember this: To know something fully, you must also know its opposite. To become unstuck, you must first be aware of what it feels like *to be* stuck.

I vividly remember the first time I ever really, truly felt stuck.

I was in first grade at the local public school (it might have even been kindergarten) and these two little boys had me cornered in the school hallway, both of them trying to kiss me. They were always trying to kiss me!

I remember thinking, at that very moment and for the very first time in my little life: "I am stuck—literally!—and I don't want to be here. I will not stay here. I will do something to change this situation."

After school was over that day, I went straight home and told my mother, "I'm changing schools. I want to go to the Catholic school down the street from us. I need a better place to be."

I knew what I was talking about. I *knew* there was a better option—I'd seen it with my own eyes!—and I knew that I was going to find a way to make this better option work in my own life.

On my way to my public school each morning, I'd always see these neat, organized little Catholic school students walking in neat, organized clusters on their way to their neat, organized classrooms for a day of neat, organized learning, inspiration, and structured fun. I wanted that structure for myself. I wanted to wear those cute little saddle shoes and pretty little uniforms. I wanted to walk in single file. I wanted to feel safe and connected and valued. I didn't just want it, I *needed* it.

Needless to say, my mother didn't just listen to me—she *heard* me. She understood and appreciated the urgency of her daughter's plea. I switched schools and immediately fell in love not just with the structure, but with the values and beliefs within those walls. My spiritual foundation is still very important to me today; it is part of my early foundation and definitely an important part of my story.

There are lots of lessons woven into the fabric of this school-switching story. The first: know what you want and be willing to do what it takes to get you there. Particularly for the young leaders and entrepreneurs who are reading these words, remember to keep your eye on the prize. If a consistently untenable situation arises, handle it. Do not become complacent. Make the changes you need to make.

Another lesson: learn to enlist the support of those around you. You won't always be able to affect change on your own. Change is not necessarily a solitary pursuit; it often requires multitudes. For me, though, the only "multitude" that was required was my mother, who listened to me, who heard me, and who respected me enough to help change my uncomfortable circumstance.

Also understand this: life doesn't have to happen *to* us. We are not passive observers and innocent bystanders. No. We get to be the artists and the architects of our own fate. We get to decide which colors to throw onto our life canvas. Yes, there will be colors thrown onto our masterpieces that we hadn't anticipated—after all, crises do occur and setbacks (even minor ones) do unfold—but what we do with those colors is what counts. No matter what, it will be our portrait to paint.

As we come to the close of this chapter, take a moment to reflect. To contemplate. To listen to yourself and actually hear what's moving in your mind. Allow yourself the luxury of sitting with those thoughts for a moment before we move to the next chapter. Maybe even jot those thoughts down if you are so moved, so that you can swing back to them later.

Perhaps these questions can guide you on your reflective journey:

- What early memories can you return to that help paint the portrait of how it felt for you, even as a child, to be "stuck"?

- What steps did you take, decisions did you make, that helped you move from stuck to unstoppable?

- Do you have a circle of trusted friends, colleagues, or cohorts that can help you and/or your organization move from a stuck position to an unstoppable position?

- What early patterns, habits, and mental mindsets have been hard-wired into your brain that might be preventing you from moving from stuck to unstoppable?

- When is the last time you reached out to express gratitude to a mentor or to the important person/people in your early life who helped get you to where you are today?

To continue traveling on this path towards unstoppable—for us to see the beauty and the potential of all that stretches out before us, waiting to be discovered—requires clear-sighted vision. It requires us to remove our blinders. It requires us to move forward in our businesses, our organizations, and our lives with a sense of purpose, courage, and clarity. We can't do any of this without first being aware of our *need* to do it. Simple as that.

This concept of awareness is what will guide us quite gracefully into the next chapter.

Everything starts with awareness.

*Chapter Two*

# AWARENESS

AWARENESS IS WHERE IT ALL BEGINS.

As we step into this next room of our literary home, we'll need to fling open all the windows, take a good, long, thoughtful look around, roll up our sleeves . . . and get to work.

The operative word here is *open*.

> In both leadership and life in general, remember that the act of *cultivating constant openness* is never-ending. Whether you're trying to create an open and transparent corporate culture, nurture an open and honest friendship, or simply develop a more open and expansive mindset when you wake up each morning to greet the new day, the process itself must be intentional and ongoing.

This process is alive and dynamic; it never really ends. Fortunately for all of us, this journey towards enhanced and conscious awareness is a journey that has no final destination, and the intentional choice to propel yourself forward on this path belongs to you and you alone.

As humans, we are constantly evolving, continually improving, always making mistakes and missteps (and hopefully learning from them), and forever fashioning better ways of being, living, and leading. We must count this as good news—the fact that this process is never ending—because it serves as a reminder that no matter where you are in life, no matter where you are on your leadership and living journey, you can *always* push towards becoming a better version of yourself, and you can always help those around you become better versions of themselves as well.

This push cannot be fully actualized, though, unless and until we expand and heighten our sense of awareness. Awareness *is* openness. Openness *is* awareness. These two concepts, awareness and openness, belong to each other. They define each other.

And though what I'm going to write next might sound ridiculously simplistic and self-evident, it's a concept that most of us seem to forget to remember, so I'm going to write it anyway: to become more open, we must become, well, *less closed*. Put another way: to enhance our self-awareness, we must be aware of our need to become more aware.

*Duh*, right? Not necessarily.

You'd be surprised by how many of us—from business owners to high-ranking corporate leaders to mid-level managers to individual contributors and even budding new entrepreneurs—operate from a mindset that is closed down. Sealed off.

Locked shut. And because we already know that our mindset and our thoughts influence and drive our actions and behaviors, this closed-down mentality can have (and often *does* have) devastating consequences.

But there is another option. There is another way to think, another way to be, another way to lead, and another way to live.

Awareness is where it all begins. If we want to move from a place of being stuck to a place of being unstoppable, we must decide to decide to *become* more open and more aware.

The choice is ours.

The choice is *yours.*

———————

## It's the Moments, Not the Mountains

When it comes to awareness, here's another fact that is standing right in front of us, with its nose pressed directly onto the window of our faces, yet we so often fail to see it: *becoming more aware of ourselves ain't all that arduous a task.*

Don't misunderstand. I'm not saying that sharpening our awareness doesn't take significant effort, intention, and action—it certainly takes all three of those things—but the process should not be seen as some mystical, climb-the-highest-mountain pilgrimage that's reserved only for the most enlightened gurus. It is anything but that. Yes, this journey can certainly be seen as a pilgrimage, but it's a pilgrimage whose paths (and there are an infinite number of paths we can choose to take) belong to *all* of us, at every moment and under any conditions—particularly the challenging, how-did-I-end-up-in-this-mess conditions that so often cause us to feel stuck.

Here I'll swing back to my mountain analogy again, but from a slightly different perspective. As we set our intention on becoming more self-aware, it's easier (and far more efficient) to focus on the tiny, incremental moments of awareness that unfold in our daily lives rather than the major, crisis-riddled, often-cataclysmic moments that tend to loom before us like mountains.

Ever try to scale a 30,000-foot mountain? I haven't either—but you know as well as I do that it's no easy task. Such is the case with pushing past crisis: it is by no means an easy task. But if we start by focusing on the tiniest, incremental moment of a crisis as we're living it—the "gentle foothills" of the crisis, if you will—it's much easier to begin the journey upward.

Moments, not mountains. Baby steps, not gargantuan leaps.

All of this requires heightened (and deepened) awareness, of course. I'll use myself as an example.

As a mom, particularly when my children were younger, there were certainly moments when I could *feel myself* becoming tense, defensive, and generally unpleasant to be around—and because I was aware enough of myself, my surroundings, and the situation itself, I was usually able to pinpoint the precise moment these feelings of discord began to surface. Because I was able to stand in the middle of those moments, as uncomfortable as they were, I was also able to change their trajectory.

Long and short of it: my awareness of those incremental moments enhanced my personal choices. Even with my kids circling around me asking for snacks or spilling juice or maybe just being the beautiful, sometimes-bickering, boisterous kids that they were, I was aware that I could choose to react to my emotions in a different way. A better way. A more pleasant way.

Had I not been aware of my own behavior in those moments as they were happening, had I not been in close touch with my emotions as they simmered and brewed and bubbled up within me, I would not have been able to choose another way. To put the brakes on the stressed-out trajectory I was taking. To turn left instead of right. To resist the magnetic pull of anger, frustration, and fear and choose a different emotion instead. To press the reset button. This was (and is) a constant effort—and even though I try to be aware of it, I am not always able to keep my emotions in check *all* the time . . . but the point is that I at least try to make the effort.

Similarly, as a leader and senior executive, when I find myself in the middle of a moment that is filled with stress, anxiety, and the never-ending pressure to perform at maximum capacity and at breakneck speed, I always have the option of making an intentional shift in my mindset, which in turn allows me to make an intentional shift in my behavior and my actions.

Awareness brings clarity of thought. It allows me to *know myself* better, to understand what drives me, what disturbs me, what paralyzes me, and (this is an important one) to understand what can propel me through the dark and difficult situations.

It all starts with awareness.

Today, I suppose, I am blessed with the awareness that I am more aware! I suppose this could be called emotional and spiritual maturity—and it happens over time as we lead and as we live. Those small, incremental moments grow into days, and

those days grow into months, and those months grow into years
. . . and before you know it, a lifetime has amassed, and what
has amassed along with it is this beautifully enhanced state of
awareness. It is an ever-evolving yet very deliberate *process*.

The other benefit to a deepened state of awareness is that it
has a beautiful "trickle-down" effect. My own enhanced awareness trickles down to my team members because it shows them
what awareness looks like and feels like. In a corporate culture,
our employees turn to us not just for organizational leadership,
but for the opportunity to model themselves, in the healthiest
of ways, after the people who guide and grow them.

Your employees, your colleagues, your superiors, your children, the people you mentor—*everyone* is looking to (and looking *at*) you, waiting to see how you will react in an unpleasant
situation, how you'll respond to an unexpected challenge, how
you compose and comport yourself in the face of a sudden and
severe turn of events. As leaders, we are looked to for guidance
and inspiration, so how we react to the world around us is
significant. It's important. And how we react to the external
world is dictated, primarily, by how well we know ourselves
*internally*.

What set of values and beliefs stand at your solid center?
(And I'm referring here to something far more expansive than
religious beliefs.) What river runs through you that creates a
steady stream? A constant current? A consistent state of "being"
that remains strong and unchanging even in the midst of the
worst crisis and the darkest day? The answers to these questions
are the answers that will ultimately reveal how intimately you
know yourself, not just as a leader but as a human being living

and thriving amongst other human beings. *So know thyself* . . . everything else will flow from there.

The good news is that awareness can be taught. It can be acquired and honed, like the skill that it is. Awareness is not just an attitude—it is a vital tool that will help you survive, thrive, grow, and embrace change in ways that you've never imagined. As a leader, you must make sure that you are encouraging your people to do the work that's involved with understanding, from a deeply personal and healthily human perspective, what motivates them to do the things they do. They must understand (and be aware of) what feeds and facilitates their frustrations and anxieties. They must appreciate the fact that their thoughts and emotions are made manifest in their actions.

Perhaps most importantly, they must understand that these thoughts and actions—particularly when they're negative or debilitating—can actually be dismantled and redirected. But conscious choice is a necessary ingredient in this recipe. Again, this requires us to focus on *moments of awareness*, on the moments we're living right now rather than the mountain that is looming before us, waiting to be climbed.

Recognizing these moments is what makes all the difference; this is the only way we can redirect their trajectory.

Case in point: Fairly early in my career, I remember presiding over what turned out to be a fairly tense budget meeting with a few members my staff; perhaps twenty people were in the room. If you're an executive, you already know that budget meetings can often become tense; it's almost the nature of the beast—but the beauty of *this* beast is that it can change. It can be controlled. It can be tamed, tempered, managed, and minimized.

We might not have control over the external events that threaten to destabilize us in life (or at work), but we *do* have complete and constant control over how we react to these uncomfortable events. This control lives right within us; it lives in the midst of our own awareness. With enhanced awareness, inner chaos can transform into calm, constructive dialogue. With enhanced awareness, negative nattering and potentially combustible conversations can be transformed into manageable, even meaningful moments that can actually lead to growth and understanding—which is exactly what happened in this meeting.

During the meeting, one of my team members became increasingly agitated as he spoke, increasingly frustrated and irritated. We've already discussed how our emotions and thoughts manifest in our behavior, and it was clear from this person's behavior—from the tone and tenor of his voice, from his facial expression, from his body language, and from the way he was making everyone else in the room feel—that discord was swirling all around (and within) him. The more he interacted with the people in the room, and the more irritated he became, the more negative energy and angst flowed through the room, like a rushing river.

But here's why this meeting is the Perfect Case Study in Awareness: Right there on the spot, right there during the meeting, this person took a pause for the briefest second. He took a breath. And within the space of this brief breath, he gave himself the opportunity to assess what was happening *as it was happening*. It was like a chain reaction. He was behaving in a way that wasn't optimal, and the "pause" he created in that moment allowed him to see himself as his behavior was occurring. This

honest, on-the-spot self-assessment—this conscious awareness—
is what eventually led to a change in his behavior.

Let's go back to the word we used at the beginning of this
chapter: *openness*. It was his openness and honesty that allowed him to hear that small inner voice inside of himself that
was whispering, "Look at yourself in this moment! Stop being
a jerk! Straighten up and fly right. Respect the humans in this
room and stop letting your extraneous emotions dictate your
behavior. You have a choice to behave differently. So, make
that choice and change your course of action."

Right then and there, in the middle of the moment, he took
a breath, gathered himself, and said aloud to everyone in the
room, "I'm sorry I am being such a jerk right now. I'm under a
tremendous amount of pressure, but that doesn't give me the
right to behave like I am behaving. Forgive me."

Immediately, the energy in the room changed.

Each one of my team members suddenly felt like they could
breathe again, because their colleague, in his previous actions
and behaviors, had been sucking up all the oxygen and energy
in the room. But when he stood before them and made his
open, honest admission, it showed everyone in attendance,
with shining clarity, that he was aware enough of his behavior
to be able to change it, to redirect its course.

With his own brush, he'd painted the glorious portrait of a
person who was able to stand in the middle of their own uncomfortable moment, as it was happening, and say to himself,
"Wait a minute. My behavior right now is allowing me to be the
worst version of myself I can possibly be—not the best version.
I will make another choice, right here and right now."

Without awareness, he would not have been brought to this point, to this glorious moment of self-assessment. *With* awareness, he was able to move himself from a place that held him horribly, irretrievably paralyzed, effectively rendering him inert and uncontrollable, to a place of clarity, control, humility, and—yep, you guessed it—radical honesty and openness.

This is what happens when you constantly cultivate and consistently nurture a heightened sense of self (not a heightened *ego*, mind you, but a heightened sense of *self*, which is an entirely different): you give yourself permission to stand in an uncomfortable moment and make the conscious decision, the deliberate choice, to react in a way that feels right to you and also respects and honors the people around you.

Awareness should be seen as a gift, a gift to be cherished and held dear at all times. A gift that will keep giving and giving and giving, in every conceivable capacity in your life—as you lead, as you live, and as you move from one simple moment to the next. But this gift only exists if you cultivate it. If you take care of it. If you polish it up and keep it shining—bright and alive and vibrant—all the time.

What better a gift is there in the world than the gift that comes from within? What better a gift is there in the world than the gift that affords us the luxury of managing our mindset and taking ownership of our behavior?

But this gift is not merely for you. It's not merely for me. It's a gift we can give to the people we lead within our organizations, and the people we live with in our families and our personal communities. By setting ourselves as examples, by manifesting and modeling the very behavior we want to see in others, we can teach others to become more self-aware, more in tune with their mindsets, and ultimately more in control of their actions and behaviors. I want to say this part again: *this is a gift we can give.* We can give the gift of heightened awareness—or at least give others the tools to access their own awareness. (They themselves will have to put in the actual work, but when they do, positive byproducts and tangible benefits will blossom like a lotus flower and these benefits will be felt by multitudes.)

Such benefits are real. They are evidence-based and statistically significant. When individual and collective awareness increase in the workplace, productivity rates increase, attrition rates decrease, employee engagement flourishes, and a general sense of well-being begins to bloom and blossom (again, like the lotus flower) throughout the organization.

So, in a very real sense, the subject of self-awareness is far more than a gauzy, somewhat amorphous, "feel-good" concept: It is good business. It is smart strategy. It yields sustainable, quantifiable results. It brings bottom-line benefits to your organization. *Period.*

But back to the budget meeting.

There are concepts and themes that live within this particular "jerk"-in-the-budget-meeting example (*his* words, not mine) that are vital and valuable. Concepts like *ownership*, *personal accountability*, *self-assessment*, and the vital importance of *emotional honesty*. I'm sure you have countless examples of your own as well, if you take a moment to reflect on them. I hope that you not only reflect on them, but write them down.

When was the last time you took ownership of an uncomfortable moment and changed its trajectory? When was the last time (or maybe even the first time) you remember your own openness and self-awareness helping you navigate a difficult situation? Take a minute to give these questions some thought; weave these questions into the fabric of your own leadership. Internalize and customize these questions in a way that allows you to make them relevant and applicable in your own leadership life. Only you know how to do this in a way that fits best for you. Are you willing and prepared to stand in the midst of the incremental moments yet to come, the moments that are waiting for you to experience, and come face-to-to-face and toe-to-toe with your own awareness? Again, it is within these incremental moments where *growth* lives. This is where the capacity to change and the momentum to move from stuck to unstoppable is waiting for you.

It is waiting for you in these moments, as they are happening.

*In the moments.*

Not in the mountains.

---

## The Six Inches between Our Ears

Here's another important lesson as it concerns the ongoing process of cultivating and growing our awareness. Though the benefits of increased awareness are vast and far reaching—virtually infinite in their scope and boundless in their capacity—it all starts within an impossibly small, teeny-tiny space that's only about six inches wide: the six inches between our ears.

It's this "headspace" that we must expand—those six small inches that span from one ear to the other—because, ironically, this squeezed-in, super-small space is where we tend to get ourselves into the most trouble. Within our thoughts. In the midst of our own mindsets. In that furiously spinning, hamster-on-a-wheel momentum we create as we navigate our busy, distracted, results-oriented lives as leaders.

> Staying stuck inside the space of our own head—and deluding ourselves into thinking that we can find happiness, prosperity, and power outside of ourselves rather than within ourselves— is one of the most tragic mistakes we can make.

At the same time, though, remember this: our own thoughts, values, and belief systems *live within us*, so staying in close touch with the things that unfold within that six-inch space is also important. Staying within that space without staying stuck in it, and knowing ourselves intimately—these are the keys. The beauty is in the balance.

Many years ago, I knew a person who always wanted to be somewhere other than where she was. Try as I might, I couldn't get through to her that regardless of where she was—whether it was Tampa, Tulsa, or Toledo, you name it—if she wasn't balanced, connected to, and in touch with that six-inch space between her ears, she wasn't going to be content.

This is a topic I often address in my speeches and in my role in executive leadership. What's most important is finding balance within ourselves *first*. Hop-scotching from place to place, site to site, location to location, is not going to bring balance, peace, and inner equilibrium.

Whether you're in California, Kansas, Canada, or Connecticut (or even Boise, Idaho!) remember that you're still with yourself. Nurture the fertile soil within your own six-inch garden before you branch out and try to transplant yourself to greener pastures somewhere else. The six-inch space must come first. It's what's on the inside that counts.

Still, though the balance is beautiful . . . it also requires energy, commitment, and dedication to maintain. If you stay stuck in that space, if you deny yourself the benefits and growth that come from expanding your headspace, you increase the risk of getting—and staying—stuck. So being aware of this oh-so-small, six-inch space is imperative . . . but so, also, is our need to push beyond it when the situation dictates. Learn to do both; learn to live and dwell in both places. Maintaining this beautiful balancing act requires discernment. It requires intentional, higher-order thinking. And it requires something else—you've already guessed the word—it requires *openness*, the ultimate gift.

———————

## The "Start, Stop, Continue" Exercise

There is a pleasingly simple, three-step exercise I often employ in my own life that helps bring me back to my center, back to the solid core of myself. Whether it's in my capacity as a senior executive or as a mom, a friend, a spouse, or a human being who is simply trying to live her very best life, this exercise helps guide, ground, and grow my self-awareness.

I've taught this technique to countless groups of other professionals, to people I have mentored, to friends who ask for advice, and even to my own children. If I had to describe it in a nutshell, I'd probably call it something like The Great Awareness Enhancer.

It's a series of questions, really—three succinct and refreshingly simple questions that you can ask yourself at any given moment during the day; the answers to these questions will help lead and guide you moving forward and will help you move from stuck to unstoppable. It is the first of many such tools and techniques I'll be sharing with you in this book.

These questions—not just asking the questions but doing the work that's involved with listening to and developing the *answers*—have anchored me when I'm feeling untethered, brought me clarity and calm in the midst of chaos. And in both my leadership life and my home life, they have motivated me in my constant quest to become the best version of myself I can possibly become.

Ask them of yourself and really *listen* to the answers that come from your heart. It is fitting and appropriate that we bring this chapter to its graceful conclusion by posing these three questions here; they will serve perfectly as our end-of-chapter reflection:

# Start, Stop, Continue

Since this book is largely directed towards leaders, entrepreneurs, and senior executives, we'll frame these three questions in a way that appeals directly to this audience—but please understand that this exercise can be utilized by *anyone* who's interested in exercising their "awareness muscle" and developing a deeper understanding of what motivates their mindset, what drives their thoughts, and what, ultimately, informs and dictates their behavior.

Particularly in our busy, priority-filled, precisely measured lives as leaders, we rarely have the opportunity to ask ourselves the reflective questions that bring us back to the basics, back to ourselves, back to each other, back to a place where open, honest self-assessment can propel us forward. Want to place yourself and your team members on a path towards enhanced awareness? Begin by asking yourself these three *action-oriented* questions:

## 1. START

If there is a gap and/or a deficiency within and amongst my team members, what are the things that we should START doing to address this deficiency and to fill this gap? (Note: This could be a gap in knowledge and/or practical experience, a gap in technological expertise, a gap in productivity and/or employee engagement—the list is infinite, and can only be defined by you. I cannot define it for you.)

Remember that as a leader in your own space and within your own organization, *you know best* how to customize and retrofit this question so that it applies directly to you. You must make these questions applicable to your own leadership life, which requires—you guessed it—enhanced awareness!

## 2. STOP

What are some of the not-so-great things I am doing with my team members—the things I might be subconsciously teaching or modeling for my group—that are actually counterproductive and destabilizing? What steps do I need to take to STOP myself from repeating these patterns? What mindset do I need to achieve that will allow me to take a pause and course-correct?

Example: Holding too many meetings with too many people in attendance seems counter-productive, and the participants do not seem engaged. This tells me that I must develop a better alternative.

## 3. CONTINUE

What are the practices and principles I must CONTINUE that are helping my team members and bringing bottom-line benefits to my organization? What things am I doing, as a leader, that are making my team members stronger, more confident, and more productive?

Example: The "lunch-and-learn" sessions are productive, stimulating, and energizing, so I know I must *choose to decide* to continue with those, because they bring benefit. Similarly, we have a robust reward and recognition program in place that really resonates with employees because it helps ensure they feel valued, heard, and appreciated. We must continue that. What *other* things must be continued?

*Note:* The "Start, Stop, Continue" exercise is useful because, if nothing else, the very act of asking these three questions sets the wheels of awareness in motion. But don't just ask the questions . . . listen for the answers as well.

As we move into this next chapter, as we enter into the next room of our literary home, we'll begin to do a deeper dive into the specific practices and processes that can help move us from stuck to unstoppable.

We've laid a solid foundation for our home, then, with *awareness* sitting at the solid center of this foundation. We are aware, now, of the vital importance of our own awareness, which is where everything starts. We understand the constant need to assess our thoughts, to understand the origin of our actions, and to appreciate how our mindset can be made manifest through our behavior. We recognize the need for reflection and self-assessment. We are ready to enter into all of the individual rooms that will give us the practical tools we need to move forward.

But let's revisit this subject of reflection. Let's push open the door to *this* room and explore the purposeful act of reflection in a way that allows us to look at it with renewed awareness.

Here is the door, waiting to be opened.

Take my hand and let's open it together.

*Chapter Three*
# REFLECTION, NOT PERFECTION

## Adjoining Rooms

YOU'LL REMEMBER THAT I BEGAN OUR JOURNEY, at the very beginning of the book, with the highly inspirational stuck-to-unstoppable story of Trina Spears and Heather Hasson, two ordinary humans, both registered nurses, who founded the extraordinarily successful healthcare apparel company FIGS. They sold the very first prototypes of their medical scrubs from the trunk of a car—and when the company went public a few years later, it was valued at more than $6 billion. A success story indeed.

Trina and Heather will be our brief touchstones in many of the subsequent chapters, because their journey exemplifies and beautifully illustrates many of the concepts we'll be exploring in this book. Their human experience helps bring these stuck-to-unstoppable concepts to life; this is why I often refer to their amazing-but-entirely-achievable success story as a real life example of living the unstoppable mindset. We'll let Trina and Heather guide us into this next room of our literary home.

This chapter should feel like an *adjoining* room, really, given that it's positioned very closely to the room from which we just emerged, where we explored the importance of awareness. I'll explain why.

Awareness and reflection are closely related, so they *should* be closely positioned next to each other. One cannot be successfully and authentically achieved without the other. Being able to place yourself in a space of reflection, contemplation, and radically honest self-assessment *requires awareness*. If you're not aware that you need to reflect, you won't spend time reflecting!

If this concept weren't so simple, it would be complicated. Awareness and reflection depend upon each other to survive— and if *you* are to survive, thrive, grow, and evolve, you too must learn to stand in the midst of both awareness and reflection. It is contextually and sequentially appropriate, then, and a very intentional act on my part, to place these two chapters—these two rooms—so close to one another.

So, let's step into this adjoining room. Fortunately, we don't have far to walk.

Emerging from the room of awareness, as we just did in the previous chapter, perfectly positions us to enter into this room of reflection.

Which means we are exactly where we need to be.

———————

## Learn to Listen to Yourself

Trina and Heather would not have been able to actualize their dream had they not reflected upon that dream *first*.

They not only reflected on it, though—they talked it through. They absorbed and embraced all the possibilities. They allowed the depth and breadth of their own human experience (rather than pie charts and bar graphs and statistical projections) to guide them as they moved forward. Being nurses themselves, they knew, better than most, what would be required to improve the comfort, durability, functionality, and aesthetic appeal of medical scrubs, simply because they wore them each and every day! And they were constantly surrounded by others—their colleagues, friends, and fellow medical professionals—who could also provide valuable input and feedback based on *their* own human experience!

Equally important, as Trina and Heather reflected upon and conceptualized their idea, they never allowed themselves to wallow in uncertainty or fear. It was this absence of fear, this refusal to be intimidated by the looming darkness of the unknown, that gave them not only the space but the *permission* they needed to let their imaginations and their creative, innovative spirit run free.

Both women had a sense of heightened awareness, and it was this awareness—the awareness of what was driving and motivating them, and the awareness that their own experiential wisdom, instinct, and intellect would be enough—that moved them forward. That they were able to remain in a reflective, self-assessing mode for as long as it was necessary only accelerated and solidified their path to ultimate success.

Trina and Heather listened to their inner voices. They felt comfortable and confident in the moments of pause and reflection that they'd created for themselves, and they saw (and valued) these reflective moments, embracing them as a necessary part of achieving their dream.

The act of reflection and contemplation is what allowed them to really listen to their inner voices. I imagine this is the voice they might have heard whispering back to them:

"You can do this. You don't have to be afraid. Think it through. Take the time you need to feel, to think, to assess, and to simply stand in this wide-open space where the only thing that exists is the purity and promise of your idea, waiting to be born . . . then put one foot in front of the other and let your journey continue!"

Trina and Heather listened to their voices, and they made damned sure that their inner voices spoke to them only in tones that were positive and forward-moving; they made sure that their inner voices were infused with a confident, "can-do" sensibility rather than a doubting, daunting tone. They knew that, at every moment, they were in control.

What gave them this measure of control? The solid awareness that, well, that they were *in control*, and that whatever happened next would happen as a result of their conscious choice.

Never once did they hold themselves to the unrealistic (and unattainable) belief that their design had to be perfect before it could be executed. They were both completely confident and completely comfortable standing in the empty, fresh-air space of their own, imperfect dream, in the space of *possibility*.

Perfection was never, ever their goal. And this freedom gave them even more freedom.

> There's a lesson here. As a leader, try to learn to listen to your inner voice more acutely and with more intention.

For so long, we've conditioned ourselves, either consciously or subconsciously, to listen to an inner voice that tells us, "You're not good enough. You're not smart enough. You're not competitive enough. Your co-worker down the hall is going to get that promotion instead of you, because they are more deserving of advancement."

Or the equally disturbing and discordant voice that whispers, "Strive for perfection at all times and expect the same from everyone around you. If you fail at anything, large or small, major or minor, it proves that you are, indeed, a failure. Anything less than perfection is unacceptable."

Or perhaps it is the voice that whispers, "Don't waste time reflecting and thinking. Spend your time doing and executing! Reflection is mindless work; it is not results-oriented and does not contribute to the bottom line. Quit all this endless thinking and use the time to act instead."

I am here to remind you that you have a deep-seated, untapped, intrinsic energy within you that can totally redirect the tone and tenor of those negative inner voices. I've trained thousands of people, all over the world, in how to listen to themselves differently, how to choose the positive voice over the negative voice, and how to train (and re-train) their brains to become more pliant, more reflective, more accepting, and less judgmental. Rebuke the negative self-talk and choose something better. This will put you on the path from stuck to unstoppable.

Here's the thing about perfection:

Perfection is a myth.

It is a lie.

It is an aberration.

It is a phantom.

It is a wisp of smoke that will always and forever elude your grasp.

I've known this essential truth about perfection—or more appropriately, this *lie* about perfection—for as long as I can remember. It's how my mother raised me, to believe that everything I was as a human being was everything I would ever need, and that as a human, I was inherently and beautifully flawed, which made me even more fabulous.

> Understand that perfection is not your friend; it is your mortal enemy.

And what's more, even the *idea* of perfection is toxic. So be careful with it. Striving for perfection is neither a noble task nor an admirable goal, though so many of us have been conditioned to believed it is both.

When I was growing up, I already knew this. As I was entering college and the workforce, I knew it. And while I've always appreciated healthy competition—whether it was competing to

get on a cheerleading squad or being the absolute best team-
mate I could be, or later on, as a rising and then senior executive
in some of the most well-respected corporations in America—I
continuously and consciously carried within me the truth about
the lie. Perfection is poison.

The vital difference in my approach to being the very best
version of myself that I could possibly be is that I never strived
for perfection: *I strived for excellence.* Being aware of the dis-
tinction is life-changing, life-defining . . . and life-saving.

> Understand this: you are your own
> competition.

You are not in competition with anyone in the world other
than yourself. The moment you begin "comparing out"—the
minute you begin to measure your success, growth, and advancement against someone else's success, growth, and advancement—is the moment you've stepped onto a slippery slope
whose only trajectory is downward, towards disappointment,
disillusionment, and destabilization.

Choosing to be excellent? *That* is the viable, admirable, even
noble path. It is the path we always want to take and, as leaders,
it is our somber yet joyous responsibility to encourage (and
train) those we lead to take this path, too. Conversely, choosing
to try to be perfect is a dangerous path. It is a path littered with
rocks, roadblocks, detours, and gaping holes. It is a path that
leads to nowhere. It is a phantom path. Do not take it. Choose
the path towards excellence.

Create a culture of positivity within your own mind (and within your organization) and choose to rebuke the destructive notion that the Road to Perfection is the only road that will ensure success and prosperity. That road does not exist, and if you try to take it you'll end up all turned around. Lost. Knocked off-course.

The Road to *Perfection* leads to Nowhere. The Road to *Reflection*, on the other hand, leads to growth, positive change, inner equilibrium, and ultimately, to happiness, success, and wholeness.

Next time your inner voice whispers, "You're a failure because you just failed at this project," make the choice to bring in another voice that is more uplifting.

Let me be clear here: we don't want to create organizational cultures that encourage (or even tolerate) *continued* missteps and egregious error-making—we do have measurable standards and performance expectations to which we must adhere, after all—but also understand that occasional missteps, as long as they are not continually repeated, offer extraordinary growth opportunities. The beauty lies in the balance—and with each and every one of these concepts that I will be introducing, it is this balance that we not just seek . . . but *find*.

Still, try your best not to create a culture where your employees feel like they'll be chastised, judged, or condemned if they happen to go left when they should have gone right, when they chose the blue box when they should have chosen the red one. Instead, take a more positive, proactive approach by taking a moment to *reflect* on what else might be unfolding around them that is knocking them off-course, to *listen* to what they're actually saying, and to *assess* what can be done to help guide them back onto the right path.

Notice the key words in that last sentence? (To save you some work, when you go back to that paragraph, you'll see that I'd already placed those words in italic. The operative words: *reflect*, *listen*, and *assess*.) And also understand that proper assessment means knowing to ask yourself the proper questions, particularly when your employees are struggling: Questions like, "Where are these deficits coming from? Are these employees being trained correctly, or might there be a slippage of some sort when it comes to professional development? Am I giving my people the tools and resources they need to strive for—and achieve—excellence?"

The questions are important, yes, but the answers that come back are equally important, which leads to the next mini-lesson: if you're going to begin listening to yourself more closely and with greater intention . . . you must first make sure you're telling yourself the right things!

---

## The Residue of Failure

I want to return, for a moment, to the Lie of Perfection.

I want to dig a little deeper into the unintended, horribly damaging effects that can—and do—result from falling into the trap of this perfectly imperfect little lie. When we ascribe more value to the pursuit of perfection than we do to the pursuit of *excellence*, things are bound to get messy. More than messy—things are bound to get toxic. Dangerously demoralizing. Shockingly off-kilter. Just. Plain. Ugly.

Why?

Because when we put ourselves in the position of shooting for a goal that does not exist (perfection), we are bound to fall short of that goal, right? How could we *not*? We cannot obtain what does not exist . . . and if we try to, if we set go after something that doesn't really exist, we've pretty much sealed the deal on our own failure, haven't we?

It's like grasping for that wisp of smoke I mentioned earlier, hoping that the smoke will turn into something solid and substantial that we can wrap our hands around, then being disappointed when that "smoke-to-something-solid" transformation doesn't occur. When this happens, we're not only left with empty hands, we're left with the stinking, stinging residue of what we have conditioned ourselves to believe is abject failure.

This is often an unconscious choice—this unrelenting quest for perfection—that has been hammered into our psyches for as long as we have been leaders, so try not to beat yourself up about it. Let's be gentle with ourselves as we try to redefine, rearrange, and reimagine our relationship with perfection. It won't happen overnight; transformation such as this takes time. Again, it all begins with awareness and being able to reflect on what is before us in the moment.

As it concerns this toxic, bitter-tasting bile, this unpleasant residue that is left on our hands and in our hearts when we fall short of perfection—which is all the time, given that perfect does not exist—there's a story I want to share, an experience I want to talk about that aptly describes the weight, the girth, and the toxic *aftertaste* that comes when this residue falls upon us.

I'd been working furiously on a major presentation that my team would be delivering to the senior leadership within our company; these were my colleagues, but many of them were also higher in rank than I was. This was a major presentation, and we'd been working on it for about four months. The concepts that would be presented would help inform and guide our strategy for years to come. The stakes were high.

In the can-do, strive-for-excellence spirit that has always shone deep within me as bright as the sun, you will not be surprised when I tell you that we had developed an exhaustive, ninety-eight-page slide deck to serve as the visual compass for this presentation. I and another colleague had worked on this slide deck over the course of countless weeks, and it had come together beautifully as a result of our collective and thoughtful effort.

A few days before the presentation, while I was on the phone with this colleague preparing to fine tune, hone, and polish everything up, something happened. As I sat down at my desk and tried to access the file, I was met with something terrifying: *nothing.* The file was completely blank.

I must pause and pivot here for just a second to ask you a reflective question: Can you remember a moment at work when your bottom absolutely dropped out? When the earth was swallowed up beneath your feet and your heartbeat slowed to a dangerous, death-like crawl? Think back to a moment in your career—really try to call up the *very instant*, if you can—when you realized you'd made a misstep so messy and a mistake so major, that it felt like you couldn't breathe.

These extreme physiological responses are direct byproducts of our fear of failing; this is a perfect example of the ugly residue that fear—specifically, fear of failure—can leave. It can leave a stain. A mark. A mottled bruise so tender it feels like you've been burned or branded or bumped with very, very violent force.

This is what I felt like in that moment. I felt like *all* of those things. But I kept searching for the file, my desperation level deepening with every click of my mouse, my fingers trembling as they flew over the keyboard, my heart dropping down to my feet. Suddenly, I in a shower of perspiration. That *flutter, flutter, flutter* in my chest threatened to render me immobile. I couldn't catch my breath.

The ugly, paralyzing residue of potential failure was trying to swallow me whole, and I remember thinking to myself as that moment was unfolding: "Brrrrrreathe. Find your center. Get ahold of yourself. Reflect on what is before you. Ground yourself in the knowledge that you will push your way through this and everything will be okay— whether you find the document or whether you don't. You will not let the possible loss of this slide deck slide you into a full panic. Take a breath."

I listened to my inner voice, of course—because that is what I have always done—but here's something else important: I also listened to the voice of my colleague, who calmed me, who helped me explore all of the available technical options, and who comforted me with the reminder that the material itself could not be *completely* lost because it had probably been backed up in the Cloud. (Ah, the Cloud. That beautiful, invisible, oh-so-very-marvelous Cloud. That miraculous repository in the sky.)

> When you find yourself in the middle of a crisis situation, *reflect* on where you are— then push past it.

Push yourself past the paralyzing moments that threaten to leave you stuck, leave you sickened, and leave you suffering. Even in the ugliest, darkest, most unimaginably paralyzing moments when your heart is hammering and your perspiration is dripping and your bile ducts are preparing a dangerous and imminent evacuation (I won't get any more graphic than I need to; we'll just leave it at that), try to remain rooted in your solid center. That's one lesson.

> The other lesson is this: learn to trust and depend upon the people around you.

Lean into the notion that the people who work with, for, and around you are capable and efficient. As a leader, you cannot afford to isolate from the others on your team. You are not an island.

This knowledge is both liberating and comforting. Let it be the voice that guides you, particularly when the waves get high and the waters get rough. *Train your brain to dust off and wash away the residue of failure.* Remember that if you suffer a major setback, even if you fail at something, it doesn't give you permission to see yourself as a failure. If anything, it gives you permission to take a breath, reflect on what is before you, then push through that moment of paralysis to get through to the other side.

Oh—and there is one more important lesson. What I'm going to write next is indeed a bit of tongue-in-cheek humor, but it's also grounded in truth:

Always create backups to your backups!

---

## The Power of the "Uns"

As we travel through the rooms and chapters of this book, you'll often hear me reflect on the fact that a good bit of training and re-training is required of us if we want to travel successfully and authentically along the path that moves us from stuck to unstoppable. This will be a recurring theme.

We have been conditioned, as we lead our lives and as we ascend the rungs of leadership, to accept certain principles and patterns of thinking that are inherently destructive. Unfortunately, many of us have come to accept these ingrained destructive patterns as the norm; we embrace them automatically, without even realizing we're doing it—without even realizing that there are healthier, happier, more holistic patterns of being, of doing, of leading, and of living *just waiting* to be explored.

The negative self-talk and toxic thinking that I described earlier in this chapter is real. It is not just a concept or a philosophy—it is as real as the nose on your face, and we subconsciously weave this negative energy into the fabric of our daily lives every single day. You can choose to stop this. You can choose to break this pattern.

> By taking a moment to consciously *reflect* on the words you choose, the nomenclature you use, and the descriptors you rely on to assess yourself, you can decide to eradicate (or at least redefine) the negative energy within your emotional vocabulary.

Particularly after experiencing a crisis (or while standing in the midst of one) the words we would use to describe our condition are often filled with what I call "The Negative Uns." Consider these adjectives:

- UNinspired
- UNable
- UNapproachable
- UNcertain
- UNfair
- UNfocused
- UNwilling
- UNcooperative
- UNpleasant

But what happens when we decide to flip these "Uns" on their head and transform them, instead, from negative to positive? What happens when we make the conscious decision to press the reset button and choose to change the downward spiral of our emotional vocabulary so that suddenly, we are using more positive descriptors like:

- UNshakeable
- UNflappable
- UNbroken
- UNbent
- UNconditional
- UNconventional
- UNderestimated
- UNapologetic

Oh, and here's one I'd like to give to you as a gift: UNSTOPPABLE!

So what happens when we decide to flip these "Uns" on their head? What happens is our lives change. This requires an intention shift in our narrative, and it requires us to listen, listen, and listen some more.

## Learning to Listen to Others

For my entire life, I have always been interested in not just in listening to but in *soliciting* the voices and ideas of others, particularly those who have suffered extraordinary setbacks and have somehow moved from stuck to unstoppable.

Throughout the course of my career, I have traveled the world interviewing many such people, conducting substantive research and amassing significant empirical data that helps me, and will hopefully help you, better understand how resilient people are able to bounce—and in many cases, even bounce *back*.

I've studied and interviewed former prisoners of war. Survivors of abuse and human trafficking. People who lost it all, then built it all back up with grace, dignity, and—very often—even with humor. With a graduate degree in change management and leadership and decades of hands-on experience, I have always been obsessed with cracking the code to unstoppable.

It is the resilience, the determination, the grit, and the undampened spirit of these subjects—these humans—I have interviewed that has helped inform and guide me as I've developed these theories and concepts about how we can move from stuck to unstoppable.

These interviews and practical research, conducted over decades, have helped teach me what I know about moving through crisis—that, and a life of my own that has been beset with setbacks, struggles, and crises. The voices I have heard over these years have deepened my own character and provided a North Star that has guided my professional and emotional development.

Let the voices of others guide and propel you on your journey as well.

This is how we grow. This is how we learn.

This is how we must live.

If these brave, beautiful people can move from the negative "Uns" to the positive "Uns," then certainly we can make similar movements in our life journey as well. Right?

Right.

---

This next golden nugget I offer up might help you shift your focus as well; this simple reminder could help tip the scales in your favor, finally, from negative to positive.

To move the needle on these "Uns"—to place yourself on another path that is more positive and more affirmative—remember to focus on what you can control. Do not focus on the stuff you cannot control; it will only contribute to a downward spiral and, thus, increase the decibel level of all that negative nattering in your psyche. *Focus on what you can control.*

When you wake up to a dreary, rainy morning, for instance, you don't focus on trying to figure out how to stop those drops and bring out the sun, do you? No, you don't—because you know you cannot control the weather. Instead, you focus on what is within your control. You focus on how to *prepare* for that weather. On what garment to reach for (hint: a raincoat!) and which tools to grab on your way out the door (another hint: your umbrella!).

Focus on the things that are under your control. And more than anything, learn to rebuke the negative labels you automatically and instinctively stamp onto yourself.

Just because you think certain things about certain things doesn't mean that those thoughts are correct or accurate. In fact, very often they are NOT.

I am reminded of a bumper sticker I saw on the back of a car a few years ago. It was a dreary, rainy day, and the sky had just opened up above me. To make matters worse, it was a morning that I was already feeling doubtful, alone, afraid, and uncertain. I was feeling disconnected. Rain was coming down in sheets, and in that moment my tears began to come down too—if not in sheets, then in sad, slow-moving rivulets down my sad little cheeks. So I pulled to the side of the road.

That's when I saw it—the bumper sticker.

To this very day, I still believe that my eyes were guided to that bumper sticker at *the precise moment* I needed to read the words. Five short words that pulled me back from the brink of a rare moment of negative self-talk and served as a reminder that just because I *think* something doesn't necessarily make it so.

Next time you're feeling untethered or disconnected, perhaps these five words might serve as a reminder that your emotions, when you feel them, are neither right nor wrong. *They are just emotions*, emotions that should be honored, yes, but not given more authority over your life than they deserve.

I'll share those five words with you now:

"Don't believe everything you think."

Amen and amen again.

---

## No Time for Nonsense

I'm going to switch gears here for a minute and dig down deep, to the topic of death and dying.

It's ironic, actually, to realize how dramatically a single death can totally transform—and forever alter—a single life. Or to be a bit more specific, perhaps I should say that it's ironic to realize how a single death can transform *many* lives.

Perspectives shift. Awakenings occur. Essential truths are revealed. Bottoms drop out and new bottoms are eventually created. So much of the stuff that we once considered important suddenly becomes insignificant and miniscule. Believe me when I tell you: death makes life more precious.

When my husband died, as I mentioned at the outset of this book, my vision changed—and I mean that figurately as well as literally. After I was able to process the raw, ravaging shock, and after I'd made sure I was able to protect and provide for my small children, my vision *did* change: It got clearer. Sharper. More acute. I began to see life differently, both at home and at work.

Though I'd always cherished the time I spent with my children, my husband's sudden death lit a Mama Bear flame within me that was as fierce and fast-spreading as the wildest wildfire. In the days and weeks after the sudden death of my beloved, my top priority was protecting my two little cubs. There was nothing more important to me than protecting them, providing for them, and encircling them with white-hot love and long, warm hugs.

But as my sudden shock grew into quiet acceptance, I entered into a period of self-reflection that I realize, looking back on it, helped save my life. You might remember my earlier descriptions of this intense period of self-reflection—how I pulled away from activity with others, how I spent hours alone, hiking, praying, journaling, praying some more, digging down deep to tap into that river of inner strength that I knew was within me, waiting for me to access it. It was these moments of reflection, these purposeful pockets of stillness and meditative contemplation, that eventually helped push me through to the other side of my grief.

Understand that the act of "pressing pause" did not suddenly remove my sadness. It did not magically make my grief go away.

It simply created—and connected me to—a deeper reservoir within me that allowed me to breathe again. To stand where I was. To honor my emotions in a way that didn't necessarily dissolve them, but that put them in a more expansive and manageable perspective.

From the moment of his last breath to this very moment that I am writing these words, a window has been open that allows me to ascribe extraordinary value to the act of reflection, to the power of the pause, to the cessation of activity. I have no more time for nonsense.

My husband's death, as earth-shattering as it was, gave me the gift of greater discernment and greater enlightenment. It helped me realize that life is too precious—and too fleeting—to waste time with empty gossip, negative thinking, and meaningless minutia.

> Leaders—if you are not actively fighting against a workplace culture that permits gossip, backbiting, professional jealousies, and petty sniping, then you are falling woefully short in your job as a leader. Learn to reject this nonsense—all the petty office politicking—and demand that your employees do the same.

Remember this: Life is precious. Time is precious. So use both wisely. When we wake up in the morning, we all have the same twenty-four hours stretched out before us, waiting to be lived. It's up to us—it's up to me, and it's up to you—to determine how best to use those twenty-four hours. Those hours, the hours that comprise the time you live and the time you lead, make them *count* for something—and not only expect but demand that the people in your organization treat their time and energy with equal respect and, yes, with equal reverence. Anything less is unacceptable.

Another point I want to make here about the fleeting nature of life itself: we often allow ourselves to become so *anesthetized* by the comforts of our regular rhythms, and we become so stuck in the familiar structure of our daily—almost Pavlovian—patterns, that we forget to push forward towards our desires and our dreams. It takes effort and intention (and courage!) to force ourselves out of our comfort zones, but when we do? Oh my! When we push ourselves into new spaces of growth and self-discovery, we are able to find more of life's rich treasures and gifts. We only have one life. One shot. One never-ending series of shots, I suppose I should say, to continually evolve and change.

Don't let life pass you by. Hold onto it tightly, even when it threatens to buck you off like a bull at the rodeo, and ride it for all it's worth! Don't be a passive bystander. Become actively involved in your own destiny. Yes, life is fleeting . . . but for the moments that we *do* remain, let's make them count. Let's live every single one of them with intention, purpose, and an eye towards being brilliant and amazing. Take a moment to reflect on this, to reflect on the fact that it is possible to become stuck even in a *comfort zone*! Try not to let it happen to you.

Becoming more reflective gives us the space we need to deepen our emotional intelligence. It gives us the glorious gift of self-assessment without judgment. It offers us the human luxury of *being*, rather than always *doing*.

All of this feeds directly back into the notion that, in order for us to be responsible, compassionate, effective leaders, we must be aware. And we cannot be reflective without being aware. These concepts are not strictly sequential . . . but they are comfortably scaffolded—meaning that one flows into the next with grace and relative ease. As leaders, we *appreciate* such scaffolding, don't we? We appreciate the structure and sequence. So, incorporating these scaffolded concepts into your daily life will be easier than you think . . . but to do it, you must do it. You must put in the work.

As you reflect on the priorities that you've set for yourself as a leader—not just a leader in your organization, but perhaps a leader in your community, a leader in your family, a leader of your own, individual *destiny*—remember that you are always in control of your own narrative.

> You might not always be able to control the plot twists and the sudden turns in your life—life is predictably unpredictable, after all—but you *can* control (and hone) your ability to embrace whatever life throws at you with grace and dignity.

If life throws some nonsense your way—and by this I mean if the people who surround you begin to make bad choices or act irresponsibly or attempt to drag you down into the dirty games of office politics and back-biting ridiculousness—don't just put up your mitt and catch it.

Throw it *back*.

Fling it away.

Toss it out of your ballpark.

Life is too short for the nonsense and nay-sayers.

I, for one, simply don't have time for it.

And if you're a good leader . . . you shouldn't either.

———

As we come to the close of this chapter, after having flung open every window and having stood in the midst of this "reflective room," ask yourself a few essential questions: How can I create a sustained, intentional effort to become more reflective—and encourage my team members to do the same?

In the quiet, still, moments of reflection and contemplation, what do my thoughts tell me? And am I able to redirect those thoughts if I realize that they have become negative or self-defeating?

Am I better today than I was yesterday? And if I can't answer this question in a thoughtful way at this very moment, will I make time to sit down, press pause, and create the mental space I need to listen—really listen—to the answers that will eventually come?

Because I've been teaching these principles to others for a very long time—to thousands of other leaders and professionals throughout the course of my career—I can tell you that the answers *will* eventually come.

They won't come during the busy, distracted moments when you're managing projects, analyzing statistics, or processing data. They will come in the quiet, contemplative moments, in the pockets of purposeful peace you create for yourself. This is why you must create those contemplative moments as often as you can.

You'll become a better leader when you do.

## *Chapter Four*
# VISUALIZE THE PRIZE

As we step into this next room of our literary home, I want to start by asking you a question: Can you feel the gentle scaffolding between these chapters?

My hope is that your answer is yes.

My hope is that yes, you can feel the *intentional synchrony* between each successive chapter, and that yes, you're beginning to understand that each of these principles flow, one into the next, in a very purposeful pattern.

The rhythm is real.

By that I mean this: we cannot stand in this new room and explore the principles (and the vital importance) of visualization—not in any meaningful, down-down-deep way, that is—without having *first* examined the importance of reflection, of being more reflective as we lead and as we live from day to day. And we cannot become more reflective in our lives until— you guessed it—we heighten and maximize our overall sense of awareness.

I know I've mentioned this purposeful pattern in previous chapters, but I keep coming back to it because it's important enough to keep coming back to. Once you understand the gentle, chapter-to-chapter scaffolding within this book, you will be better able to ascend these scaffolds in your life as well. These principles are *alive*; they don't simply exist as words on a page—they are *built* for you, as living concepts, so that you can customize them in a way that fits most comfortably into your own life.

The deeper we go into this book, the more tangibly you should be able to feel the structure of this scaffolding, and the clearer it should become to you that this structure, and these principles, really do build upon one another—not in a strict, intractable sequence, but in a very graceful and gentle unfolding, like the unfolding of that beautiful lotus blossom I described in Chapter Two.

And now, we climb a little higher.

As we ascend this next scaffold where we examine how best to *visualize* our dreams, our desires, our goals, and our lives, we ascend towards a more expansive mindset; a mindset that allows us to view all that exists and all that is *yet to* exist, waiting to be discovered.

Let's turn to Trina Spear for moment. Let's examine how she was able to move her idea of improving the quality and practicality of today's medical scrubs from a wisp of a wish to an actual image in her mind!

That's the thing about visualization: whether it's a company waiting to be born, a product waiting to be developed, or a fresh, new career waiting to bloom and blossom, it must, by definition, begin in an empty space, where nothing yet exists. There must be a gap that needs filling. An empty patch of fertile soil that needs planting. A spark that needs igniting. An *itch*, if you will, that needs scratching.

Same with Trina. Maybe as she was putting on her scrubs at home one morning, or on her way to the hospital, she noticed that itch. A *literal* itch. Perhaps the tag on the inside of her shirt scraped uncomfortably across her skin. Or maybe, as she was grabbing her keys and dashing out the door, she had the fleeting thought, "I sure wish I had a *pocket* to throw these keys into!"

Who knows? Perhaps her "Aha!" moment came—and this is pure conjecture on my part—as she was standing in front of her mirror and a thought bubbled up: "I need some *color* in these scrubs. I need a bit more functionality. What I'm seeing before me doesn't necessarily have to be how it remains. I see something different for myself!"

The point is this: somewhere along the way, Trina Spear expanded her mindset and allowed her brain to visualize a nurse's uniform that *did* have pockets and that *didn't* feel scratchy and that *could* look cute and be fun and functional all at the same time! She allowed her mind to take her there, and in doing so, she effectively moved her mind from an itch . . . to a scratch. And that "scratch" reinvented the $60-billion medical apparel industry as we know it today.

This is what visualizing your goals, picturing new ideas and possibilities, and breathing the breath of life into all those empty spaces, into all of those gaps and holes, can do. Not only can it fill you with a spirit of determination, but it can actually allow you to throw vibrant colors onto the canvas of your life.

"To see it is to be it," then, is not just an empty aphorism. It is a concept that is alive . . . and it is waiting for you to pick it up and bring it to life.

---

## "Seeing" Your Way through Crisis

When a crisis occurs, or even a series of mildly uncomfortable moments, you've no doubt heard people talk about the importance of "seeing your way through," right? It's a common part of our vernacular, particularly in crisis-ridden situations.

But it wasn't until my husband's sudden death that I really, truly, fully, authentically embraced the emotional accuracy of these words—and I mean I embraced them with every fiber of my being and every ounce of strength I had within me. What I realize now is that this ability to "see your way through" a crisis is what saved me (and my two small children) from a dangerous downward spiral.

I've already described in earlier chapters how the days and months following Howie's death threw me into a toxic tailspin. I am not at all ashamed or embarrassed to admit this, because standing in the middle of *those* moments is what guided me to the very moments I am living today.

Today, I am healthy. I am balanced. I live a vibrant life surrounded by a loving family, and I enjoy long, meaningful friendships. I am a dedicated and deeply engaged leader who moves and motivates others. I love and I am loved. My point is this:

I wouldn't be here, in these moments today, unless I'd pushed past those paralyzing moments I experienced and endured earlier; those painful moments are responsible for bringing me precisely where I stand now.

Remember this as you face your own challenges and your uncomfortable moments: you will push through them . . . if you keep your eye on the prize.

During my own white-hot periods of grief and loneliness though, in those days after Howie's death, it was the practice of visualizing myself in a different mental space that really helped get me through. Visualization is what helped me align myself more fully in the present, for the sake of my children if nothing else. I knew that if I was going to be present for (and protective of) my little ones in a way that they needed and deserved, I needed to purposefully place myself in some mental space other than my own abject grief, other than my own paralyzing pain.

It was this "vision" of another way, another way of being and behaving, this act of literally *seeing my way through* to another emotional and mental space, that helped me navigate my own heavy-as-concrete grief—a good thing, too, because that grief was sucking all of us down into the molten earth like quicksand. There was no other choice. My children were depending on me. The mere awareness that they needed their mama more than anything was what moved me towards greater mental clarity.

As leaders, we can see our way through difficult moments.

We can visualize ways that lead us out, detours that lead us around, pathways that lead us under, and windows that open onto new solutions, simply because that is what we are trained (and paid) to do, and that is what we *must* do for our employees.

To be able to see your way through a crisis or a setback requires you to open your eyes and see the world around you with clarity, courage, and a wide-eyed sense of professional and personal accountability. Remember: *you are built for this.* You have it within you. As humans, we are built to survive; it's in our DNA . . . but it requires that we dig down deep, to places we're not accustomed to digging. It requires that we use mental muscles that have never really been exercised before. This is what will allow us to step onto a higher plane of functionality. But it takes work. Effort. Intention. Don't let this daunt you; let it energize you, this knowledge that everything you already have within you is everything you will ever really need to survive, thrive, lead, and live a meaningful, happy life.

As leaders, we must continually remind ourselves, remind each other, and remind (and empower) our employees to access and embrace this innate capacity that exists within each of us.

As a mother of two young children whose hearts were hurting, though, what I knew I needed to visualize was a world for my babies that was more orderly, more structured, and more intentionally cleared of the chaos and the clutter that had been surrounding us in the shocking aftermath of Howie's death.

I want to share a story. About two years after that tragic accident and after our world changed forever, I received a promotion that required us to move across the country, from Phoenix to Delaware. My children were still deeply traumatized from the sudden loss of their father, and I was, I realize now, not just experiencing my own trauma, but I was experiencing their trauma as well, in a sense. How is such a thing possible?

Because their grief was imprinted upon me in the most unexpected moments . . . watching them wait for the door to open and for their father to walk through it, for instance, or seeing their little eyes searching for their papa when it was time to sit down at the dinner table—it was these micro-moments of my *children's* grief that laid a new layer onto my own.

Plus, their angst and anxiety morphed into deeper angst and anxiety at the thought of having to relocate yet again. Change was not their friend; the last time they moved, their father died. I could almost see their beautiful little minds swirling with worry and weighty questions like, *Who's gonna die now that we're moving again? Will my new teacher and friends be nice or not so nice? What will our new bedrooms look like? Will we lose our mommy like we lost our daddy?*

I will make this admission, too, with no shame and no embarrassment: When we arrived in Delaware, I didn't do a great job of creating an environment that felt structured, secure, and safe. I realize it could have been better.

My brave young son felt this absence of structure.

He felt it with such intensity that even then, at barely five years old, he let me know that the anxiety of this constant disorder was *getting* to him. He let me know he needed structure again, a sense of solidity, a sense of order. Being his mother's son, he said as much, straight out—and the mother-child confrontation felt like a cold but necessary slap in the face.

One bright Monday morning, he looked at me, face red,

eyes brimming with tears, and screamed at the top of his lungs, "Mom! What . . . is . . . the . . . AGENDA . . . for . . . the . . . Day? What are we DOING?"

The very next day, I erected a flip chart in our dining room. I answered my son's urgent plea. I created a visual for him—for all of us, really—that guided our activities and ordered our steps. Using brightly colored markers, I wrote down the activities we'd be doing that day:

"6:30 a.m.: Wake up. Have a good breakfast!

7:30 am: Drop the kids off at daycare and at school.

8:00 am–6:00 pm: Enjoy the day! Mom picks us up.

6:30 pm: Dinner and relax.

7:00 pm: Bath time.

7:30 pm: Story time with Mom then lights out.

The point of this exercise was that we were able to visualize a daily goal—step by step, hour by hour, minute by minute—and in visualizing this structured sequence, by writing it down and claiming it as tangible and real, we were able to create order out of chaos. Tranquility out of turmoil. We were, in the most literal sense of the word, able to *see* our way through.

Looking back on this visual timeline reminds me of something else too. As a hard-charging VP, I usually didn't pick up my children until at least 6 p.m. each day—that's a long day for me, but an even longer day for them. The lesson in this, and it's a lesson learned in retrospect given that I didn't (because I couldn't) absorb it as I was living it out: setting boundaries and clear expectations with others (and even with ourselves!) is crucial, necessary, and healthy . . . so don't forget to set them!

I was so focused on the never-ending work-related tasks

in front of me, so pinned down by the "busy-ness" of my relentlessly non-stop work schedule, that I neglected to set the
necessary boundaries I needed to set that would get me home
at a decent hour.

> Let the lesson be this: in your constant
> quest to move up, to meet (and exceed)
> what is expected of you as a senior
> executive, and to constantly ascend those
> ever-present "higher rungs," don't forget
> to set boundaries for yourself.

Remember that you cannot be everything to everyone at
every time, and in moments when your family needs you, you
must do what is necessary—cut a few corners, perhaps miss
a meeting or two, try to pick the kids up from school before
the *sun sets*, for goodness' sake—so that you become more
present in their lives. Find a way to bring yourself back to the
people who depend on you and on whom you depend. Let that
be a lesson. Boundaries are vital, they are also oh-so-easy to
overlook. Do not overlook them.

Because of my son's heightened awareness, and because of
his ability to reflect and assess the situation at hand (which
had become, to him, untenable), and because he knew, even
at that young age, that something had to give, he was able to
request—no, *demand*—a visual tool to help him through.

Leaders, you can provide these tangible tools for your employees as well. Help them see what it looks like to go after a

goal, step by step, incremental moment by incremental moment, and give them the vision they need to get them there.
Leaders need to be open enough—aware enough—to hear what
their employees are asking for. They need to be listening and
looking, mindfully and with intentional precision, for the signs,
for the red flags. They need to be opening their hearts so that
they hear the calls for help when (and if) they do come . . . and
then they need to be able to take swift, decisive action.

It is said that if you ask for it (whatever "it" may be) with a
sense of urgency, you will receive it. My son certainly asked—
and he asked with urgency.

Because he asked—and because I was open to seeing and
hearing him *when* he asked—he received.

---

## Collective Vision Is Crucial, Too

Remember that our visualization doesn't always have to be—
*shouldn't* always be—focused inward. As humans, we must
resist the urge to constantly train our vision on ourselves and
focus solely our own advancement, to the exclusion of all else.
This ego-driven, me-me-me mindset creates tunnel vision; it
narrows our perspective and slaps the blinders on, giving us a
dangerously myopic view of the world itself and our connection to it.

As leaders, we must remove those blinders and seek a more
expansive view of the world around us. This requires us to
visualize not just our own success as we ascend the corporate

ladder or picture our own victories as we continue our ascension upward; we must also lay claim to and paint a picture of the more expansive growth of the employees we lead, the customers we serve, and the communities in which we live and work.

An organization whose leaders don't have a clear, consistent vision of their company's goals, mission, and values is an organization whose leaders are not visionary at all, but stuck in the revolving door of their own drive towards success.

Make sure the people you lead share your larger organizational vision and are able to articulate and "throw paint onto the canvas" of that vision in a way that is demonstrable and consistent. Your ability to sharpen that collective vision is every bit as important as your ability to sharpen the picture of your own personal and professional goals. Put another way, make sure you're seeing the larger picture and not just your own. Collective vision is crucial.

Here's an example: I first started working for Disney at a very young age, as an intern working at the Walt Disney World property in Lake Buena Vista, Florida. I was wide-eyed, open-hearted, and boundlessly excited about working for one of the most spectacular companies on the planet. But even at that entry-level position, still a teenager, I was quickly and immediately made to understand that the company had a very strong vision of—and for—itself, and that nothing should get in the way of communicating that vision to its guests.

If there is such as a thing as being Perfect in the Art of Visualizing a Company Culture (we know there's really no such thing as perfection, but we'll leave it like this because it's so much fun to imagine), then Disney wins First Prize.

When it comes to an organization that understands its vision, communicates that vision, and demands that this collective vision and shining corporate culture be shared by each and every one of its employees—then constantly shared with the customers—Disney is the hands-down winner. They get the blue ribbon.

A funny story: At one point very early in my Disney career, long before I began to ascend the management ranks, I worked as an "Attractions Hostess" at Epcot, which meant I was in a "guest-facing" role that required I work directly with the paying public. In this capacity, I was often called to stand onstage and introduce the film the guests were about to watch. I should add here, that this was a *speaking* role; I had lines I actually had to deliver.

The very first time I took the stage, I hadn't really prepared as thoroughly as I should have. I hadn't exactly memorized my lines. And as I stood onstage and looked out at all the expectant faces—faces that were fully expecting to feel the joyous sensation of the Wonderful World of Disney showering over them as they sat back in their chairs and prepared to watch the movie—something awful happened: I dissolved into a fit of giggles.

I couldn't stop laughing, couldn't catch my breath. Heck, even if I *had* memorized my lines, I wouldn't have been able to deliver them, so consumed was I by the torrent of giggles that kept bubbling up and splashing forth. Well, you can best believe that my manager wasn't *about* to tolerate some young intern standing up on stage placing even the *slightest* smear on the company's Sparkling, Beautiful Brand. No such nonsense was about to occur, then or ever. No sir.

Immediately after my embarrassing onstage moment, my manager met me backstage and promptly shared his "vision" of what the corporate standard was—and that standard, as you might imagine, was precise, exacting, and immovable. It included a perfect presentation (or as close to perfect as one could get, anyway), well-memorized lines, well-practiced vocal inflection, and even carefully presented hand gestures and always-bright smiles. What it *didn't* include was uncontrollable giggles.

"That's not how we do it at Disney," he explained firmly. "The guests are expecting you to bring them the magic and warmth of the Disney Experience. They don't want to see or hear you dissolving into a fit of giggles. If you're feeling nervous or if you're having a bad day, work all that out backstage. When you step onstage, you're not bringing your own experience to the audience. You're bringing them the *Disney* experience. Keep that in the forefront of your vision."

That experience taught me the value of preparation and the importance of understanding—and conveying—the collective vision of an organization. The misstep actually matured me in a very real way, too. You'll remember, in the previous chapter, we examined the importance of learning from our mistakes and using those missteps to guide and inform us as we move forward. Well, my embarrassing onstage misstep helped me realize that my own ego, my own nervousness, was irrelevant; equally important, it had *nothing* to do with the larger, collective vision of the company.

> In any successful organization, one's ego and/or one's desire to be well-liked, understood, and/or accepted takes a second seat to the organization's larger corporate vision.

Sometimes you have to learn this the hard way. It's funny, now that I look back on it . . . but it wasn't all that funny as it was happening.

Another lesson is this: with each and every employee you bring onto your team, it is your responsibility, as a leader, to ensure that their vision remains in conscious, constant alignment with your company's vision, with your company's *heart and soul*. Egos be damned. As leaders, we cannot confuse our own desire for popularity and acceptance (ego again) with the larger desire to ensure popularity of the brand we are representing. *The brand comes first*. Egos must take a back seat. This is what is I mean by "keeping your eye on the prize."

As managers and leaders, we must remember that this "prize" isn't simply the pink stuffed animal we might be trying to win for ourselves at the county fair. This "prize" doesn't just belong to me. It doesn't just belong to you.

It belongs to—and stems from—the organizations we lead. The *company* vision is what drives us. And it is this collective vision that should order our steps.

## Letting Science Speak

The act of visualization is not a feel-good, hippy-dippy, sitting-around-the-campfire act of ephemeral, wistful, and, yes, *wish*ful thinking. Visualizing another path, a better option, or a brighter way to be, to lead, and to live requires real brainwork.

There is science involved. There are new neural pathways to be forged and electronic signals within the brain waiting to be sent and received. There is some heavy lifting involved. In the same way you exercise a muscle until that muscle grows stronger with repeated use, we must exercise our brain until it becomes stronger and more pliable.

This is what is often referred to as *neural plasticity*, which is the brain's capacity to modify itself, both structurally and functionally, as a result of intentional and repeated effort. With consistent use, just like a muscle, it becomes higher functioning. This is, quite literally, mental exercise. This is mental gymnastics.

The concept of neural plasticity is not new. High-functioning athletes know about it. So do stroke victims—and any other humans whose well-being and/or survival depends upon their ability to create new pathways in the brain to ensure high performance (or a return to high or at least improved performance). They know that this principle is evidence-based, empirically rooted, and directly correlated to the certainty of science. There is no guesswork involved.

The injured star athlete, for instance, who is temporarily prevented from physically bench-pressing those three hundred pounds during practice is the same star athlete who has trained his brain to *visualize* himself bench-pressing those three hundred pounds. And as he's honed this visualization technique with such accuracy, with such pinpoint precision, that when he closes his eyes and allows his mind to take him there, he will feel the same burn, experience that same breathlessness, and reap the same benefits as he would have if he were actually lifting.

How? Because as he is visualizing the bench press, his brain sends the electronic signals to his body that he really *is* lifting. These neural signals trigger an actual increase in his heart rate. Secretion of his perspiration glands. Fatigue of muscles. So that when he is finished with the mental exercise, the *physical* benefits are real. They are tangible. They are touchable.

So, yes, this is about science, but this is also about mindset. It's about the *marriage* of mindset and science—a match made in heaven.

You, too, can create this kind of mind-body marriage; it is attainable, it is neurologically possible, it is real, and it waiting to be accessed. So roll up your sleeves, open your mind, and get down to the business of making it happen.

But don't just take my word for it. I'd encourage you to dig a little deeper. Do your research. There's plenty of data-driven evidence out there that recognizes and celebrates this science-based mind-body connection. Fully inform yourself so that you, too, can make this direct connection—create this vital, living link—between your brain and your behavior.

Mindset matters.

———

## The Ocean in Front of Me, the Mountains at My Back

You know by now, having journeyed with me through this book so far, that even as a child I was a pretty high achiever, a pretty hard driver, and a person who never really hesitated to go after the vision I'd put in my head. My capacity to see myself doing what I *wanted* to be doing has always been strong.

But it wasn't until I was at Disney that I participated in a formal, structured, "self-awareness" event that really changed my life. The event, a three-day, off-site gathering, opened my eyes in ways they'd never been opened before. Powerful and profound, those three days forced me (in a good way) to dig down deep and assess my values, my core beliefs, my priorities, and yes, my future dreams and aspirations.

I remember one exercise well. We were asked to write down our "vision" on a piece of paper and describe what we saw for ourselves in the future. It didn't take long for me to make my list. The descriptors of where I *wanted* to be in the future came flowing from my pen with sure-fire rapidity. My list looked something like this:

### "I want to be . . ."

- Healthy and "centered" in mind, body, and spirit

- Living in California, surrounded by a loving family

- Motivating, teaching, and leading others

- Writing (Perhaps a *book*?)

- Sitting in my sun-splashed home office, with the ocean in front of me and the mountains behind me

Over the years and decades, I kept that list close to my heart; I settled it comfortably into my mind and visualized myself working towards those goals and one day achieving them. I didn't just visualize that list; I *internalized* it. I made it mine.

And sure enough, the list moved from being mere words on a piece of paper to life unfolding before me, in real time. Because I was able to see my success, to stand in the midst of my own growth and propel that growth in a mindful, purpose manner, I was able to direct and influence how my own reality played out before me.

If I had to make a list of what my life looks like today, at this very moment, in this space I am standing in right now, the list would look something like this:

- Healthy and "centered" in mind, body, and spirit

- Living in California, surrounded by a loving family

- Motivating, teaching, and leading others

- Writing (Yes! A Book! At this very moment!)

- Sitting in my sun-splashed home office, with the ocean in front of me and the mountains behind me

If that's not proof positive that visualization works, that mental imagery is real, and that our thoughts (that is, if we think them consistently and with great intention and follow through with intentional action) can bring us happiness and success, then I simply don't know what is. I am living today the very life I built for myself on that piece of paper almost three decades ago. And you can too.

Understand this: thoughts are *things*. They have a specific weight and heft. They are not just fleeting, wispy tendrils of smoke that escape from our brains, drift up into the sky, and—poof!—evaporate into nothingness. (Well, they *can* be wispy tendrils, but our job is to assign value and vision to the thoughts we have so that we use this mental energy in a way that actually moves us forward—very useful indeed, particularly when we feel stuck.) When combined with purposeful action, the thoughts we think and the goals we envision for ourselves and for our organizations can and do transform into great and wonderful things.

Make sure these transitions—from awareness to reflection to visualizing the prize—occur in your own life. Create your own momentum. Give your thoughts, goals, and dreams the mental energy they deserve—not just once in a while during a comfortable, quite moment, but *all the time*. Let your ability to visualize your goals become habitual. Train your brain.

Also, be cognizant of and conscientious about training others to create this momentum and to lay these new neural pathways in their own lives as well, not just with your employees, but also with the people you love and who love you, in your home, in your neighborhood, and in your communities. We *all* need this mental space. This fertile soil. These wide-open windows through which we can climb and grow and leap and discover.

What "ocean" do you visualize glimmering in front of you? What "mountains" are at your back, waiting to inspire, motivate, and move you forward?

What are your passions? Your dreams? Your driving goals and your deepest desires? (Not just your personal values but the collective values of your organization?)

What is your WHY?

If you can't answer these questions just yet, it's okay. The fact that you are asking them is what matters most. The fact that you are training your brain to expand, to stretch, to forge new pathways (literally), and, like rising water, to constantly seek a new level as it rises, should be recognized and celebrated. You are climbing these scaffolds with purpose and intention—the very purpose of this book.

Let's let the ascension continue.

## *Chapter Five*
# FIND YOUR BROOM CLOSET

We all have our own "broom closets."

We all have our own space where that *spark* ignites.

Whether that room is physical, mental, emotional, spiritual, or perhaps large enough to hold all of the above, this space holds grace. It holds the promise of action. It is a safe refuge into which you can retreat, a place that lifts you up, pushes you forward, and busts up all the bottlenecks that were blocking your flow and impeding your progress.

As we continue our journey through our literary home, the next room that we'll step into is not really a room at all. It's more of a safe little corner. An inspiration nook. A smaller, more self-contained little area that belongs to you and you alone. It's a *launchpad* of a room, really, that can catapult you into action and propel you forward when you're running low on fuel and short on energy.

This next sequential scaffold we're going to examine, this next chapter, leads us *beyond* visualization. We will be moving *beyond* the dream-making, the goal-setting, and the mental fortification that is required to push past the challenges that so often confound us. This next room moves us towards action and execution. This is the space where the doing of deeds can begin to happen; where energy flows and sparks fly. This is where stuff *gets done.*

Want to know where my first "broom closet" was located? Let me tell you.

My broom closet was . . . a broom closet.

———————

I'd started my new job as an organization development consultant at a major bank in Phoenix. My heart was still deeply ravaged and the greedy clutches of grief still had me twisted up, turned around, topsy-turvy. Plus, I was new in town—hadn't even had a chance to familiarize myself with the traffic patterns yet. I didn't know a soul and not a soul knew me. I was pretty sure the people at my new job didn't really understand (or care about) the role of—or reason for—an "organizational development consultant" anyway.

All this *newness* was numbing. I was rudderless, bobbing around in a turbulent sea with nary a compass *or* anchor.

Let me describe just how rudderless I felt: I'd been feeling so lost and alone, so disconnected and out of place, so mercilessly unhinged that I was actually thinking about tossing my two precious children into an Airstream trailer and high-tailing it the heck out of Dodge, blazing out of our driveway faster than an Indy racecar driver, burning rubber and leaving marks on the asphalt as we made our way to, well, as we made our way to *wherever.* To points unknown. To someplace other than the place we were at that moment.

That's pretty darn rudderless, I'd say.

Sure, I had a lovely office on the seventeenth floor in downtown Phoenix and the sun rose high in the sky each day, sending bright rays of warmth over that entire, lovely little city . . . but those rays never seemed to reach *me*. They never warmed me up or filled my soul or penetrated my spirit. In fact, everything in me felt cold and lifeless, like I was living in an eternal state of sunlessness and perpetual shade.

On one particular day, though, the rays of sun streamed through my office with such intensity I couldn't help but smile. The funny thing is that this "sunlight" arrived in the form of a FedEx box.

When the FedEx box arrived, I had no idea what could have possibly been inside . . . but I was soon to find out. What I found was the gift of a lifetime. What I found was a way back. A way through. A way around. I opened it carefully.

Inside, a beautiful pair of classic, black suede Gucci loafers, along with a handwritten note from my thoughtful brother, reading, "I know you're hurting, but keep both your feet on the ground. Remember who you are, and what you're made of. Walking away is not an option. One foot in front of the other. That's the only way you're going to move through this."

I placed my brother's words directly into my heart. Then I placed his beautiful gift of Gucci loafers directly onto my feet, literally and figuratively.

The very next day, putting one foot in front of the other, I walked into my gleaming office, packed up my few belongings, and transferred myself to another physical space a few blocks down the road, to the building where the business unit and team of people I was assigned to support were located.

Yes, I still worked in my position as an organizational development consultant . . . but now, I no longer cowered in my seventeenth-floor office. In this new space I'd found for myself, I found that I could push out into the sea of colleagues and interface with my co-workers more frequently and with greater confidence. Gradually, as these interactions increased, they began to understand and have a deeper appreciation for what I did—and I, in turn, began to appreciate more fully what they did, how they did it, and what drove them to want to do it every single day.

The Gucci loafers lit the fire under my feet and helped me walk away from what I now realize was something of a pity party that I'd been throwing for myself . . . but it was the physical move to this new space that also pushed me to a place of action and a place of *doing*.

> We all need to have a place to which we can retreat that helps facilitate *the act of acting and the deed of doing*, a place where the creative sparks can fly and the pistons can pump to their hearts' content, without fear of failure or judgment.
> As leaders, it is imperative that we not just find this place, but create this space for ourselves and for the people who work with and for us.

Here's the thing, though: this "space" that I'd chosen just happened to be a broom closet . . . a literal broom closet! But I could have given less than a hoot. What mattered most was that I'd found a space that somehow made me feel safe, that somehow allowed me to reinvigorate my sense of purpose and place, and that somehow—blessedly!—kickstarted my confidence back up to its original level and pushed me out of my hazy funk.

The moment I opened the door to this closet and peeked inside, I smiled inwardly, nodded gently, and said to myself, "This space will do *just fine.*"

And I jumped into action immediately.

I cleared out all the brooms and mops, dragged away all the boxes and empty containers, dusted off a little spot in the corner, pulled in a little desk, pushed in a little bookshelf, flipped open my laptop, hooked up a little lamp, sat myself down on a little three-legged stool . . . and I got to work.

The more I worked with others, the more others wanted to work with me. I began to get things done, to tick things off my list, to visualize and actualize my goals again—this time, in a way that aligned more closely with the larger, collective goals and vision of the organization itself. I no longer felt like an island. People began to notice my work and to observe the positive impact I was having on the organization and on the collective energy of the team itself.

One afternoon, the president of that particular division of the bank poked his head in and asked, "Who are you? And what are you doing in my broom closet?"

I explained to him that I'd recently, and of my own volition, "relocated" myself to this spot and that the relocation had given me the momentum I needed to get my job done more efficiently, more creatively, and with a greater sense of purpose and urgency.

We began to work closely together. He'd request something—for me to develop a document, proof a strategy statement, whatever he needed at that moment that required my expertise—and I'd have it in his hands almost before he could finish asking the question.

He'd seek my opinion and I'd give it, freely, openly, honestly, and with thoughtful intention. And if he gave me an assignment that I wasn't quite sure how to approach or complete, I did whatever needed doing to *learn* how to get it completed. To deliver the goods. To get it done and get it done well. My broom closet gave me the space I needed to regroup, reignite, and, to put it simply, kick my butt into action.

Two months later, I was his chief of staff.

My upward trajectory in the banking and corporate world continued from there. Sure, I'd been stuck. But finding my broom closet—again, not just the passive act of finding it, but the far more pro-active act of *creating* it—helped push me past stuck.

That and a pair of beautiful Gucci shoes.

---

## Customizable Concepts

There is a small basket of beautiful lessons waiting for us within this broom closet experience, all of which I'd like to share.

The first lesson is more of an affirmation than anything else. It's the forceful reminder that you too can take literal and figurative steps in your own leadership life (and your own personal life) to push yourself back onto the path where you need and want to be. This is an *innate* capacity. It exists within each of us. I want this book and the customizability of these concepts to provide you with a roadmap that can guide you onto the path of being the best version of yourself that you can possibly be. I am giving you the tools you need; it is what I am trained to do—and it is what I train others to do.

Whenever you feel like you've fallen out of alignment, been knocked off balance, or become isolated from the people in your organization or the loved ones in your daily life, you must rest in the awareness that the power to shift this dynamic rests entirely within you.

Nobody else is going to propel you into motion. Nobody else will create your broom closet. They might give you the tools and support to *lead* you there (like my brother Tim's urgent reminder to get my head out of the depths of despair and put one foot in front of the other in my new Gucci shoes) but the ultimate act belongs to you. Make the choice. Then take the actions.

Another lesson in this beautiful broom closet basket is this: learn to trust and rely upon those around you. As leaders, we tend to isolate sometimes. We have a bad habit of separating ourselves from the people who work with and for us, which is a grave mistake. We've already touched on this concept in earlier chapters, but it's worth swinging back to again simply because this "I'm-an-island" tendency is so dangerously pervasive amongst senior executives and management professionals.

The long and short of it is this: if we close ourselves off, we cannot open ourselves up—to new ideas, to continued growth, and to the joy (and wisdom) that comes from exploring and discovering new concepts and principles with others. And here I post an essential question: How in the world can you share the collective vision of your organization (which we just explored in the previous chapter) if you're standing apart from those around you?

This leadership journey is paved with vital, brilliant, capable people. Lean into the knowledge that you don't—and shouldn't—have to travel this road alone. There are people surrounding you who have the knowledge, the passion, and the creative energy to help you advance your goals and to ensure that the larger goals of the organization are constantly being observed and honored. It is natural to want to isolate when we're not feeling our best. I know; I've done it myself. But we must resist the tendency and break the habit.

I suppose another lesson here is that, as leaders, we must always be consciously aware of how easy it is to be lulled into a false sense of security, comfort, and yes, even complacency. If we're sitting in a well-appointed office, high up in the sky, soaking up the perks and benefits of the corporate life (I'm using myself as an example), it's difficult, sometimes, to touch and feel the rough areas of our lives that need buffing up, the ragged areas that have become frayed and fragmented that need to be rewoven or rethreaded.

I suppose my point is this: don't let the *trappings* of success, well, trap you. Dig down deep inside, beyond the gleaming office and the stock options and the reserved parking space on level B1 (right next to the elevator, no less) and make sure you are feeling what is moving within. If something feels off-balance, don't ignore it. Honor it. Address it. Pull it out and examine it. Become your own agent of change.

I look back on it now not with embarrassment or regret but with pride, at the memory of my packing up and walking out of that seventeenth-floor office. Understand, of course, that it wasn't just the office that didn't feel right; it was the person and the professional I was when I was *inside* that office, and even more importantly, the essence of the person that I actually was, that felt off-balance.

Taking action, then, is an inside job. It requires heightened awareness and an unflinching ability to self-assess and self-reflect. These are the very things that will lead you to the necessary and deliberate actions that will push you through. It's the *scaffolding* again, one stuck-to-unstoppable principle leading to another that eventually results in actions that move us towards a new way of living and leading and being.

Simple? Yes. Easy? No. You've got to put in the work, commit the resources, and enlist the support of those around, above, and below you within your organization . . . but this is what will lead you to unstoppable. *You must claim this as an actionable strategy.*

———

## A Broom Closet for Everyone

Another lesson—and this one requires us to remove the blinders that we so often wear on our constant quest for personal success and professional advancement: remember that this is not just about your finding your own broom closet—it's about helping others find theirs, too.

Do you recognize what your employees need as they build their own broom closets? Are you paying close enough attention to their mindset and their attitude so that when they do send you signals that they're in distress or in need of change or assistance, you are actually able to *receive* those signals and offer help? As a leader, are you doing all that you can do—*everything* you can do—to create the necessary stepping stones for your team members to grow and evolve and walk in new directions? To forge ahead on new paths? To actualize their own dreams and goals?

If you aren't, you should be. Because if you're not creating an organization culture of growth, if you're not nurturing a culture where *everyone* is seen, heard, and valued, you are not doing your job. Your people should come first. Always. It's as simple as that.

Everyone needs their own broom closet, and it's our responsibility as leaders to help guide them towards it.

-----

## Your Personal Board of Directors

I write a lot about joy and gratitude. I talk a lot about these two topics, too. Whether I'm speaking before an audience of ten or one hundred, or while formally training leaders on how to move their employees from stuck to unstoppable, conducting one-on-one leadership sessions with individuals who want to learn how to place themselves on this forward-moving path, or even in my comfortable, casual conversations with the people I love and who love me, my message is always this: Joy and gratitude abound all around us. They are not finite resources, like water or crude oil. No, joy and gratitude are infinite in their depth, their breadth, and their availability. The problem is that we don't always take the time we need to reach out and purposefully pull these resources into our lives—or to push them, intentionally, into the lives of others.

This can change. We can and must align ourselves with these two concepts in a way that is tangible and enduring. One way to do this is to recognize that you did not get to where you are today by yourself. *Look at your life!* Look at how far you've come, how many bumps in the road you've traversed, how many victories you've enjoyed (and earned, by the way), how many setbacks you've survived! Be grateful and joyous in the knowledge that you didn't get here by yourself. There was a trusted tribe of people surrounding you who lifted you up when you fell down, pushed you forward when you slipped behind, and offered their hand to help you ascend whatever rungs you were trying to ascend on your journey.

As you continue to move through life, remember this. Remember that you do not have to go through it alone, and that joy and gratitude are constantly surrounding you in immense, even infinite, doses. You just have to stop long enough to tap into them and "shut up" long enough to really hear the beautiful sound they create. It's a sound (and a song) that we don't allow ourselves to hear often enough, which is a sad and sorry shame.

It doesn't have to be. We have the power and the choice to access this joy and gratitude at any time, under any conditions. But it must be seen as a purposeful act.

It's almost like plugging an appliance into an electrical outlet. Unless you take the deliberate step of plugging that appliance into the socket—to make that purposeful connection—the connection itself will not occur, the electricity will not flow, and the appliance will effectively be rendered inert.

Without electricity, your toaster won't toast. Your freezer won't freeze. Your computer won't connect you to the living world around you. You *must, must, must,* make the purposeful connection. Without it, nothing moves . . . and all of this beautiful potential energy lies dormant. In everything you do, do whatever it takes to connect yourself and align yourself with joy and gratitude. Make them belong to you. Because if you don't have them, you cannot give them away.

Again, this is not just a feel-good, pie-in-the-sky principle. It is firmly rooted in universal truth, which tells us that experiencing and expressing gratitude and joy doesn't just make good common sense . . . it makes good *business* sense, too.

A company whose employees are appreciated, supported, rewarded, and empowered to be the best version of themselves they can possibly be is a company that will, in turn, be appreciated, supported, and rewarded by the communities and the customers it serves. Put your people before your profits and your profits, as a direct result, are far more likely to be realized. People first.

Joy and gratitude, then, belong in the High-Priority pile of any business plan or organizational construct. This is a human truth *and* a business mandate.

Isn't it wonderful, the recognition that we cannot—and should not—travel this road alone? No matter your age, your gender, your economic status, the position or rank you hold within your organization, or the color socks you select when you're getting dressed in the morning, rest easy in the knowledge that there is enough joy and gratitude to go around for all of us, and that on this often-bumpy road we travel, we are never really alone.

Even better, we have the power and the capacity to maintain fairly close control over the "tribe" of people who surround us—not complete control, mind you, but the awareness that we can make a conscious choice about the people we trust, the people we can lean on, and the people who we *know* will offer us sage advice, honest guidance, and an always-open heart and listening ear. These are the people we want to surround us, right? I'll answer that for you:

Right!

I like to call this tribe, this band of trusted brothers and sisters, this community of caring, conscientious humans who surround us, guide us, and protect us, a Personal Board of Directors. You've probably heard the term before. I didn't coin it. The concept doesn't belong to me and me alone by any means. *Everyone* should have a Personal Board of Directors. For as long as I can remember, I've always had one, and I hope that you decide to make the intentional effort to form one in your own life as well.

The beauty of this board lies in its malleability; you can switch out the members as life dictates, as situations shift, as priorities change, and as your vision and values expand or contract. And if you discover that the people on your Board are no longer in alignment with your values and your beliefs (not necessarily in *agreement* with, but in alignment with—there is a difference), you must feel free to shift the composition of your board. "Staggered terms" are a good idea—not just in the corporate board room but on your Personal Board of Directors as well! You have the control. You have the choice.

It is this board that will help guide you to your broom closet when you've lost your way. These are the trusted persons who will help nudge you back to a space and a place where your spark can reignite, your broom closet, your conscious, creative refuge, where the essence of *you* resides.

There are many precious people on my Personal Board of Directors—close family members, best friends, trusted colleagues, and mentors who have led and guided me along the way. I rely on these people at different stages and points in my life, and as the saying goes, sometimes they last for a reason, sometimes for a season, and others, for a lifetime. There was someone who always stood at the solid center of my circle in my formative years, not just because of his "can-do" mentality and brilliant business sense, but because he was one of the most creative humans I have ever known.

Especially when I was growing up, I always saw this person as an *idea* person. He was always working on something new, always conceiving and tinkering and strategizing, which fascinated me as a child. In fact, he conceived and launched many businesses in his lifetime. And I loved our conversations. Not only did he provide inspiration, but he'd also impart small gifts of wisdom to me every now and then. A favorite book here. A profound idea there. Small gifts that served to inspire and motivate.

That's the thing about having a Personal Board of Directors: sometimes you get really great gifts!

That brings up something else I want to say about this thing called the human condition: we *all* have gifts to share with one another, but it is up to each one of us to decide how these gifts will work best in our lives. We have the choice of deciding precisely how what is given to us will fit into the nooks and crannies of our daily existence. The choice is ours. The choice is *yours!*

So make sure the people on your Board actually *bring something* to your life! Make sure their gifts, should you choose to accept them, are put to good use. Conversely, if you are fortunate enough to sit on someone else's Board, make sure you bring something positive, something substantial, and something enduring to their lives too. Don't just be a bump on a log. Make your presence *count* for something.

This subject of tool-sharing and gift-giving is important. When we share tools with others to inspire and uplift them—to push them through dark moments and pull them up and out of the quicksand—we must give careful thought to the gifts we give.

The tools we share with others *matter.*

Here's a perfect example . . .

---

## The Tiffany Key

I have a very dear friend named Laurie, a former colleague and a long-standing member of my Personal Board of Directors, who unlocked a door in my life for me some years back after I'd slammed it shut with the brute force of a sumo wrestler. Laurie not only led me back to that locked door . . . she gave me the key to open it. That's what I call a true friend.

Many years ago—for a variety of reasons and as a result of a series of unfortunate (and uncontrollable) events—I'd become stuck in an unpleasant and uncomfortable emotional space.

It felt like I was swimming (no, make that *drowning*) in the deepest, darkest waters of the deepest, darkest ocean—in those frigid, frightening waters at the bottom of the ocean where the monster-like fish live and no humans have ever descended. That is pretty darned deep.

Each day—at work and at home—I felt like I was *spinning, spinning, spinning* my wheels furiously . . . without moving an inch. Worse yet, some days even felt like I was spinning, spinning, spinning, and only moving *backwards*.

Not even the safe confines of my broom closet were able to bring me peace. And I will admit this, here and now: perhaps I was feeling a bit sorry for myself, maybe I was playing the victim rather than the victor, but the truth of the matter was I didn't *feel* like a victor! And if you don't feel it, you cannot be it.

I'd mentioned to Laurie, on more than one occasion, that I thought I might need some external help, that I couldn't navigate these deep waters alone. I told her that I needed someone who could drop a deep-sea fishing line into these murky waters and help pull me up, up, up from the deep, dark depths, because my attempts to rise to the surface on my own had been wholly unsuccessful.

Not too long after this admission, I received a package at my door—yet another FedEx package!—this time much smaller than the gift of Gucci loafers from my brother—but equally treasured.

With a rapidly beating heart and short breaths, I opened the package.

Like Russian matryoshka dolls, one beautiful box nesting inside yet another beautiful box, I finally came upon a jewel of a package: a tiny box of bright, brilliant Tiffany blue.

I held it in my trembling hand. Inside, a Tiffany necklace with a silver key attached to the chain, along with a note from Laurie:

> *"You are the key. You are the answer. Believe in yourself, listen to yourself, and unlock what you know is already resting inside you."*

In this graceful, generous gesture, Laurie had done what Laurie has always done: she'd called me out, she'd opened my eyes again, and she'd reminded me that everything I already had within me was everything I needed to free myself from the vise-like grip that had been holding me hostage. She put the brakes on my pity party. She told me (lovingly) to get over myself and push past the darkness, reminding me that it was okay to stand *in it for a minute* . . . but that I'd been standing in it for too long and it was time to get moving.

This is what the valued members of your Personal Board of Directors do for you. They bring you back to yourself; they push you—sometimes gently, like Laurie, sometimes not-so-gently—back to the safe walls of your broom closet where you can retreat to reenergize, reconnect, and, if necessary, shed a few final tears before stepping back out to face and embrace the world with courage and clarity.

Who is on your Personal Board of Directors? During those difficult moments when you need someone most, who is it that you turn to? Who can you rely on to guide you towards your broom closet when you've lost your way? And are their values in alignment with yours? Do they have loving, trusting relationships with the people around them? (Because if they don't with others, then they probably won't with you.) Who are the people in your go-to tribe?

These are questions that should really apply to everyone who stands within the sacred space of your trusted circle, whether that space is occupied by the loved ones who surround and encircle you at home or the colleagues and fellow associates who surround you at work. The point is that when we do get stuck, having someone we can rely on to help move us to unstoppable is essential.

No, the onus doesn't rest, shouldn't rest, and cannot rest entirely upon another person to move you back onto the right path. The ultimate responsibility belongs to you and you alone—but this trusted person or these trusted people can certainly add momentum to your movement.

You do not have to travel this road alone.
There are others out there who can walk
with you, who can encourage you to put
one foot in front of the other (walking
in beautiful suede Gucci shoes sure
helps!), and who remind you to believe
in and listen to yourself when the noise
gets too loud.

*Look* for those people.

Create those circles of trust. Rely on this trusted band of brothers and sisters to lead you back to your broom closet if you happen to lose your way. And embrace the indisputable fact that getting lost, getting turned around, and being knocked off course is all a natural part of leading and living.

It's finding your way again that showers us with the glorious reminder that we are—all of us, when the rubber meets the road—really, truly, beautifully unstoppable.

## *Chapter Six*
# NO SILVER PLATTERS

"TAKE THE BUS."

The *one time* I ever complained to my mother about not having reliable transportation that could get me to my various jobs, and this was her three-word response:

"Take the bus."

Those three words summed up, with unapologetic grace and straightforward intensity, her approach to life and living. As a single mom raising three children on her own, she certainly ascribed to the philosophy that there are no silver platters in life. No red carpets. No free passes.

But she didn't just ascribe to this philosophy. She *embodied* it. With every breath she took, she *inhaled* it. With every deliberate move she made, she *lived* it. And she taught her three children to stand fearlessly, boldly, and happily within this life philosophy too. I still stand within it today.

In fact, this philosophy, this way of living, this intentional mindset, this conscious choice, is why I am who I am today. It is why I am healthy, humble, balanced, triumphant, resourceful, resilient, still scrappy, and yes, happily whole.

I grew up knowing that if I wanted something in life, I'd have to go after it myself—without complaint, without resentment, and certainly without the unrealistic expectation that someone else was going to hand it to me in a brightly wrapped, perfectly presented parcel. This is why, as you remember from earlier chapters, I reached out and grabbed what I wanted. I didn't wait for it to come to me because I couldn't wait for it. If I waited for it, it wouldn't come. So *I went after it.*

Whether it was bartering a deal with my dance instructor (when I was in elementary school) for free dance classes in exchange for my teaching the lower grades, or marching into JCPenney when I was homecoming queen in high school to ask the manager to sponsor my trip to a New York beauty pageant, or managing an ice cream store throughout college to defray costs, or cleaning offices when I was twelve—the list goes on and on and on—I did what I had to do to get what I needed and wanted, because if I didn't, I wouldn't get it. Simple as that. So I stood in the middle of my center and pushed myself forward to create positive change. Create my own momentum. What happens when you *don't* create your own momentum? That answer is easy.

You don't move.

If you intend on moving yourself from stuck to unstoppable, this is where you must stand—in the middle of your own, solid center, confident in the conviction and strong in the knowledge that everything you want in life—whether it's a new job, a new relationship, career growth, a renewed commitment to your own inner vision and sense of purpose, or just about anything else under the sun—is well within your reach if you're willing to put in the work.

I want to return to this word *reach* for a moment, because the act of reaching is perhaps the most vital act of all. Why? Because it's a purposeful act. It's an intentional behavior. It's a conscious decision that is born out of heightened awareness, self-reflection, and an ability to visualize what you want, followed and fortified by the gumption and the grit to go after it.

These are the very principles and practices we have explored in the previous chapters. These are the very tools that you already possess and that you have at your disposal. Joy of joys! The vital awareness that all we've learned thus far is all we'll need to reach, reach, reach for our goals and our dreams, all we'll need to push through our points of paralysis and figure out another way to live and lead! *The reach is the thing.*

When we reach, we move. We don't just sit back, complacent and expectant, and wait for things to come to us. No. We lean into life with every ounce of strength and determination that we have within us, whether it's tackling a single, challenging project at work, pushing an employee towards new levels of growth, or encouraging your toddler to try the jungle gym instead of just the sliding board at the playground . . . this is how we promote growth in ourselves and each other.

Let's linger for a moment on this subject of the sliding board and the jungle gym, because they are actually—and surprisingly!—applicable and relevant to the subjects of growth, evolution, and the power that lies within conscious choice.

Let's go back to the playground of my youth for a minute.

My mom was a busy woman, as I've mentioned. She didn't have a lot of spare time to take her kids to the playground, but when she did, you better believe she made the experience count!

The life lessons she imparted upon me, even as a child—even at the *playground*!—filtered into my soul and my psyche in ways that are permanent and palpable to this very day.

As a kid, I was always a softy for the sliding board. I loved the feeling of *ascending*, rung by careful rung, higher and higher into the sky, then swooshing down to the bottom, running back around to the ladder, and climbing that mountain again, always pushing myself upward, step-by-step, towards the sun and the sky.

It was my mom who encouraged me to try the *other* fun stuff at the playground too, thereby expanding my singular line of vision. Sure, the sliding board was fun. I could have climbed up those steps and slid down that slide for hours! But I learned that remaining in my oh-so-comfortable "comfort zone" for too long would eventually limit my scope of experience—a real shame in this case (and on *this* playground), given that so many other fun, exciting options were only a few feet away.

So one day I tried the jungle gym. Yes, I could still enjoy the upward ascension, but now, I could move in different directions as well! I could shimmy to the side or move up a rung and then down, or maybe do a fancy dismount and end up on the ground! Never before had these options been in my line of vision.

> The lesson here is that we must be careful of remaining stuck in our comfort zones, a particularly tricky lesson because of the simple fact that our comfort zones are so, well, *comfortable*!

Constant growth and positive change help us expand our horizons and widen our sphere of influence. There is, indeed, joy in a jungle gym! (To this very day, I cannot pass one on the playground without smiling and sending a "thank-you" thought to my mother.)

There's another lesson that springs from the jungle gym. When I talk about growth and professional development today in my one-on-one training sessions, or when I'm leading a group session, or even when I'm speaking to someone one-to-one, young interns just starting out, entrepreneurs, women in leadership and on the rise, whoever the audience, this is the lesson I share: Growth is not always about moving *upward*. The path to growth is multi-directional. It is rarely exclusively linear.

Think of the new manager, for instance, who's just accepted a lateral move to a new division where she will be learning new skills and exploring entirely different skill sets. This might not necessarily be a promotion in an upward-moving sense of the word, but it is sure, steady, healthy growth that will allow her to expand her base of experience and widen her sphere of influence.

This is the example I use when I'm training, leading, and speaking with others, and it's a message that I want to make sure I direct to the new entrepreneurs and young managers who are reading my words right now and might be evaluating the progress of their growth patterns: Do not look at your professional development path as a straight-up-and-down ladder. There *is* no ladder.

Take the jungle gym approach instead. Certainly, an upward trajectory can be exciting, ego-boosting, and often quite rewarding . . . but I'm going to appeal to you, right here and now, to nurture a more expansive, multi-dimensional perspective when it comes to your own growth. Resist the urge to be myopic and one-directional. Don't just slide down the sliding board all the time. Resist the urge to constantly define success and growth as an upward trajectory. Take the jungle gym approach instead.

Train your brain to find value not just in the climb up, but in the exploration and discovery that's involved in moving in other directions as well. Believe it or not, an occasional step backward might even be necessary at times, particularly when we're looking at growth and development from a healthily holistic vantage point. The optimist in me says, "One foot forward and one foot backward isn't a bad thing, it's the cha-cha!" So, keep dancing through what you think is a setback and eventually you will see it as a comeback!

Remove those blinders and reach for a more wide-open, all-encompassing lens as you look at your life and your role as a leader. Don't be afraid to move sideways, under, and around as you climb your jungle gym and navigate your path forward. Slide right! Step back! Flip around! Put one foot up and rest the other foot on a different lateral rung. Wherever you are, stand in your solid center. Learn to ascribe value to *all* directions of growth, not just to the upward climb. You'll be a better, more effective, more present leader if you do.

Understand, also, that you are responsible for the ultimate direction you take, for which rung or step you take next. Certainly, external factors play into and greatly influence your direction—the mentor who advises you, the boss who directs you and evaluates your performance, whichever members of your Personal Board of Directors have a hand in helping you grow—but in the end, the decision and the choice belong to you. The onus is on you.

What this means in the context of the "silver platter principle" is that your continued growth—not just as a leader but as a constantly evolving human being—must remain in perpetual play as a result of the momentum you create. Don't sit by and expect things to happen. Don't get deluded by a sense of expectation (real or imagined), or by that always-slippery sense of entitlement.

Instead of expecting that promotion to come your way simply because you've tricked yourself into thinking "it's my turn, and I deserve it," ask yourself, *What should I be doing to win this race and get myself across the finish line? What actions do I need to take? In what ways can I hold myself accountable for my own reality and growth? What am I doing to move my own needle?*

This is about mindset more than anything. As a leader, you must remain eternally vigilant and vitally aware that your employees stand in constant need of growth. This doesn't mean that they have to switch jobs every quarter or that their job descriptions need to be rewritten every month, but it does mean that we should be on the constant lookout for opportunities to help expand their experience and push them towards greater opportunities for self-discovery.

When you are leading teams of people (or even a few individuals) let them know that they are being heard, they are being seen, and that they are valued. As a result, they will develop a stronger and more abiding sense of self-worth, which results in greater job satisfaction, which in turn results in greater engagement, higher productivity, a more meaningful connection to their customers and distributors, and on a greater scale, a deeper, more enduring sense of purpose and connection.

This is higher-order thinking that stems from something elegantly simplistic: the desire and intention to be kind to one another, respectful of one another, and consciously aware of a shared vision that includes growth, expansion, and continual improvement—not just on an individual level but on an organizational level as well. Put your people first. The profits will follow.

Teach your employees the value of being flexible, accountable for their own actions, consistently resourceful, and firmly grounded in themselves. From this will spring the awareness and understanding, on their part, that what they do, what they say, how they behave *matters*—not just on a personal level, but as a reflection on and contribution to the overall organizational culture and collective well-being. When everyone is held accountable, and everyone wants and expects to be held accountable, misplaced expectations and that dangerous sense of self-entitlement seem to fall away. Understand that there is a direct correlation.

Don't permit your employees to rest on their laurels or slip into automatic pilot and glide on in to that next promotion. Help them understand, through your own actions and behaviors, that silver platters do not exist, nor do red carpets. No cruising allowed.

I, for one, never had the luxury to cruise—not even in elementary or high school. My mother wouldn't let me cruise. It was never an option.

I took the bus instead.

## The Quest for Quiet Confidence

As we move into this next room in our literary home, it might begin to feel like we're climbing the stairs to the upper level now. Up here, we will open the doors and windows to even higher-order concepts and principles. They will still be firmly rooted in the reality of our everyday existence, of course, but they will have an elevated feel, because now we can begin to incorporate all that we've seen in the previous rooms, all that we have read and absorbed in the previous chapters, into our larger frame of reference.

Put simply, our *knowledge* has been elevated . . . which allows us to see things not just from the ground level, not just from an introductory, "first-floor" level of understanding, but from a higher level of understanding as well.

As we arrive at this second level of our home, then, we are perfectly poised to explore some of the higher-order concepts that come into play when we talk about how best to move from stuck to unstoppable. We've already talked about essential leadership traits and characteristics like self-confidence and accountability. But now we can enter that quiet place within us, where these traits and characteristics actually *live and breathe.*

I want to bring us back to this notion of "quiet confidence."

We all know it when we see it: that manager, executive, business owner, or just that humble human being who wears their self-confidence wrapped around their shoulders like a comfortable cloak. You know people like this. Heck, you might even *be* one—the kind of person whose beliefs, values, and unswerving sense of self seem to flow from within before spreading outward to touch everyone around them.

There's an *aura* surrounding these people—an energy field—that ripples and runs through them like a bubbling spring, and if you're anywhere in their vicinity, you feel it too. What is the "it" I describe? I like to refer to it simply as *quiet confidence*, rooted in an unwavering faith in one's self.

This is mindset stuff. This is the living, breathing acknowledgment that if you are to truly soar to your highest heights, you must develop and nurture a way of thinking, a way of being, a way of leading, and a way of living that is firmly rooted at your solid center. You must believe in yourself and embrace the awareness that everything you have inside you is everything you'll ever really need to make the changes you want to make in your life.

This doesn't mean you can't reach for and implement new tools and resources to enhance your journey, such as the principles and concepts we've explored in this book. In fact, my hope for you is that you take what you've learned during our journey and weave the threads that are most resonant to you into the fabric of your daily life. It's ironic, really, that the concepts I share are so universal in their depth, breadth, and applicability, yet they can also be so uniquely customized to fit the contours of your own human experience. Universal and unique, simultaneously.

> The fact of the matter is that our growth—and our capacity to help others grow—starts as an inward journey. You cannot help others develop more expansive mindsets if you do not know how to develop a more expansive mindset of your own. You cannot teach what you do not know.

This leads us right back to the principles of self-reliance, personal accountability, and being able to take ownership of every single aspect of our lives. This is an inner journey, an emotion-based journey, that starts with how well we know ourselves, how much we trust ourselves, and how much we believe in our own capacity to grow and evolve.

*This* is where that quiet confidence is born—from deep within. Eventually, it travels outward so that the people around us can see it and feel it as well. This is the best way to reach (and teach) your employees, your business partners, and your colleagues.

It is your duty as a leader to create and nurture an organizational culture in which the people around you, the people who depend on you and learn from you, see with their own eyes essential personality characteristics like self-confidence, a strong sense of personal accountability, unswerving integrity, and an abiding belief in one's self.

When they see how these patterns of belief and behavior manifest in you, they begin to understand how these things can live and breathe in their own lives as well. They begin to understand that their growth and development stems from their ability to *go after it* and put in the work. Sitting idly by, expecting things to come your way, waiting for that Perfect Plan or for that beautifully ornate silver platter to be handed to you—those are not realistic or healthy options.

It is entirely possible—and again, it is our duty as leaders—to help our employees learn these inward-turned concepts and to embrace, with every ounce of their being, the notion that *if it's going to be, it's up to me.* This is not just a catchy aphorism. It is an essential belief that can be acquired, nurtured, and activated!

I also want to emphasize that this quiet confidence of which I speak is not just an ephemeral, elevated concept that hovers somewhere in the sky beyond our reach. It is not a concept that's been sprinkled with magic dust and must remain shrouded in mystery and mysticism.

It is not that at all.

These concepts and principles are rooted in reality. They are tied to the world around us, whether that world is comprised of the four walls of your office, where you're interacting with and leading your employees, or the walls of your home, where you interact with the people you love. My point is that *this stuff is real.* Yes, these are elevated concepts indeed, but the fact that this is higher-order thinking doesn't make it any less real. It just means that our thinking, as we have traveled together, room by room, throughout each chapter of this book, has become more expansive. We must count this as a good thing.

Similarly, the concepts of ownership and accountability that we've been exploring are not just feel-good concepts. They are directly tied to real life, and there is a direct correlation between strong self-confidence—that quiet confidence that comes from within—and successful leadership. Particularly when we're feeling stuck, it will be this quiet confidence that helps move us to unstoppable.

This is what we must nurture in ourselves before we can teach it to the people around us! This is what lives within the silent folds of quiet confidence—and these are the lessons that you must teach your employees, the lesson that confidence is attainable and that it is necessary for personal and professional growth.

Maintaining this constant sense of personal accountability and ownership is what will keep you from sliding down that dangerous, slippery slope of having unrealistic expectations; it will hold the "Silver Platter Syndrome" at bay. Be *consistently confident*. Train your brain and manage your thoughts in a way that allows you to tap into this self-confidence when you need it most: when you're feeling anxious, disconnected, inadequate, and afraid. When you're feeling stuck, you must turn inward *first*—not outward—for sustenance, strength, and forward-moving momentum.

Reach for it. Dig deep. It's waiting for you. This sense of self-confidence and inner balance belongs to—and comes from—YOU. Tap into it and bring it out so others can see it and be inspired.

Wear it around your shoulders like a comfortable cloak.

———————

## Leading Others to This Light

Although internalizing these concepts and activating them from within is the necessary first step, what comes *after* that is equally important: being able to spread the good word to others that we must hold ourselves accountable for our own actions is vital and necessary.

In my own life, for instance, spreading this good word comes in many different forms—in my one-on-one coaching sessions, for instance, or when I'm leading large groups of executives and senior managers. Often, I spread this message to others in the form of a soft nudge, a gentle reminder, or in the space of a quiet, private conversation.

My children, for instance, have heard the constant refrain from me that success, growth, and positive change will never just be handed to them. Moreover, as they reach for what they want in life, for what they need, for the meaningful things that sustain and fulfill them, they must root themselves in the awareness that the choices they make on the paths they choose belong to them—and that these choices have consequences.

As they matured, gained autonomy, and grew into thoughtful humans, they always knew (as they still know now) that I won't tell them what decisions to make. Of course, when they were very young I had to make decisions for them—that's what a mother does for her children, after all—but even then, I always wanted them to understand the impact of decision-making and the power of conscious choice.

As young adults today, it's important that they understand that their decisions are *their* story. The onus is on them to make their own, conscious choices, just as the onus is on you. But my children also know that I will always be there for them to talk through the *consequences* of their choices. And I am confident that they have the internal navigational devices—that vital "inner compass"—they need to guide them through the challenges and choke points that will invariably come their way.

In my own family, this No Silver Platter principle has crossed bloodlines. It has spanned generations. It has leapfrogged over time and place to become something of a family legacy. My mother gave it to me as a gift, and I have, in turn, passed this gift of awareness and enlightenment on to my own progeny. And hopefully one day, when the time comes, they will pass it along to theirs.

This is proof positive that these principles can not only be internalized . . . they can be externalized and pushed forward into the world as well. They can be taught, transferred, shared, and given as precious, enduring gifts to the people around us.

How will you share these gifts? How will you convey these principles of personal accountability, integrity, and ownership to those around you in a way that they can understand, internalize, and actualize?

In addition to quiet, comfortable conversations with the people I love, the other way I spread this no-silver-platters message to people is by simply being aware enough, present enough, and discerning enough to gauge when people are stuck and might be in need of a nudge.

> This is an important leadership
> characteristic to develop in your own life:
> a sense of emotional openness will allow
> you to look more insightfully into the lives
> of others—but be careful to look without
> harsh judgment, without sharp prodding,
> and without heavy-handed (and often
> unwelcome) advice.

Learning to be fully present brings benefit not just to you but to the people around you. I'll share an example with you from my own life.

I make fairly regular visits to my favorite holistic wellness center. Doing so brings me balance and tranquility; this place of peace brings *me* peace. It helps me remain present and available not only to the people around me, but to myself, so that I can think more clearly, visualize more vividly, and stand in my own mental space with greater clarity and intention.

During a recent visit, as I was getting a massage, I noticed that the owner of the center seemed unusually tense; her vibrational energy felt, to me anyway, a bit frayed and frenetic. I looked at her more closely and noticed that her face was even a little flush. When I asked her if she was okay, a conversation began that quickly (and comfortably) evolved into open, honest sharing in which she really communicated to me some of the issues that she was grappling with—business issues that were weighing her down and causing her great concern.

We were able to *talk it out*—and I was even able to offer her a few ways to tweak her business model that might bring greater benefit. The point is that because I was present, because I was aware of her discomfort, I was able to gently and directly reach out and inquire about her well-being. This opened the door to a deeper discussion in which feelings were shared, emotions were identified, and practical, next-step recommendations were offered. Because we were *both open* to a conversation like this, we were able to connect some of the dots. Fill in some of the empty blanks. Evaluate some fresh, new possibilities that she hadn't yet considered.

Next time I saw her—which was only about six weeks later—she greeted me with a warm embrace and a tearful, deeply felt expression of great gratitude. She thanked me for coaching her, for taking the time to reach out, and for being aware enough in that moment to ascertain that she might need a bit of help or a warm word.

But not only that. She'd been able to incorporate some of the business-related strategies I'd offered her, and it had made an almost-immediate and very dramatic difference! This was the perfect example of one human being helping another human being move from stuck to unstoppable. The perfect example of one person taking another person by the hand and leading them through their stuck point. The perfect example, I should also add, of a person (her) who refused to wallow in her own discomfort, who refused to play the victim, and who was ready and willing to hold herself accountable for pushing herself towards positive change . . . and then *did* it.

This is what accountability and ownership look like. And the fact that I was able to make a difference, to act as something of a catalyst during her crisis, shows that we are able to help each other push through. We can lend a listening ear, an encouraging word, and a little guidance and expertise. It makes a difference!

Here's what kind of difference it made, specifically: In the less than six weeks, she was able to more than double her revenue. She was able to quit her second job. She was able to expand her retail space to accommodate the dramatically increasing demand, and her rebooking rate was through the roof!

Awareness. Reflection. Openness. Action. The refusal to stay stuck. These are the tools, the principles, and the practices we have learned, together, as we have moved through the chapters of this book.

How will you internalize and solidify these principles in your own life so that you can push them outwards to those who will benefit from your wisdom and enlightenment? What steps will you take next?

How will you breathe the breath of life into these concepts in your own life so that you can then pass them to those who are standing, at this very moment, in equal need?

## *Chapter Seven*
# RIDE THE WAVE

LET'S DO A QUICK VISUALIZATION EXERCISE. Imagine this:

You have hit your stride. Your life as a leader is deeply fulfilling. You are teaching and motivating your employees in ways that facilitate their continuous growth and the growth of your organization.

At home, your connection to the people you love and the people who love you is strong and enduring. You are a vital, visible member of your community, helping your neighbors, supporting your local businesses, and maybe even coaching your kids' soccer team.

You donate to causes close to your heart with comforting regularity. You volunteer at the local senior center, reading books and engaging in meaningful discussions with the seniors who live there, and you do this on the regular, not just when the mood hits you. They *need* you, and they look forward to your visits.

You are even doing the important *inner* work—generating positive thoughts, creating moments of stillness for reflection and contemplation, maybe a hike in the hills or a cup of chamomile in the kitchen before your busy day begins.

There's a rigor and rhythm to your life, a groove. You feel *connected*. Complete. Confident. Content. Happily whole.

If this scenario sounds like it might be describing any aspect of your life as you are living it today, I want you to stop for a moment—I mean, put this book *down!*—and give yourself a little hug of appreciation and gratitude.

Take a second to stand in the shining awareness that your life today is balanced and meaningful. Do a quick, reflective, self-assessment and say to yourself, "Yes! My life *is* balanced and meaningful (for the most part, anyway) and for this awareness alone, I am deeply grateful."

Take this important moment—no, *create* this important moment—of awareness, affirmation, and gratitude. Feels good, doesn't it?

Now, let's take this level of awareness to an even higher level. You certainly have the tools you need to ascend to this new level—you have the capacity—because we've traveled together through all of the rooms in our literary home, chapter by chapter, exploring each of the stuck-to-unstoppable principles. Now we stand here, ready, willing, and totally prepared to ascend to the upper levels of our home, where even higher-order thinking can unfold. (Take yourself back, yet again, to the image of the lotus blossom unfolding.)

We move now beyond just a general sense of gratitude, to a place I like to call *cause-and-effect* awareness. Rather than just feeling gratitude for a life that is balanced and meaningful, stand in the awareness that your life is balanced and meaningful because you've put in the work and made the consistent effort to *make it* that way! Because of the conscious choices you've made and the deliberate actions you have taken, you have created a life that you love. Stand for a moment in the awareness of this *cause-and-effect* correlation. It is real.

The life you are living now is not passive or benign. The reason that you are "riding your wave" is not because of some faraway, mystical alignment of the planets above. No. It's because you have taken the steps to get to precisely where you stand today. Again, there is a cause-and-effect correlation between where you stand now and the steps that you took to get there—and this growing awareness places us on a higher plane of consciousness. Revel in this awareness. Honor it.

But let's climb a little higher still, onto the next level of mental and emotional clarity, by asking ourselves a few important questions:

What happens *next?* What steps do I need to take, what moves do I need to make, that will deepen and expand all of this goodness? Yes, I'm out here surfing on the beautiful waves of this vast ocean around me, but how can I ascend even higher to get an even *better* view of the world around me? Equally important, do I have the tools I need to get back up on my surfboard if something happens and I'm tossed into the sea?

The questions themselves guide us gently to a very important piece of knowledge: that even when we seem to be at our *pinnacle*, even when it feels like we've reached our apex and are cresting every wave that comes at us, it is still possible to get stuck! Even when you feel like you're at the top of your game, humans are capable of getting tripped up, knocked down, and tossed around a bit . . . simply because we are human.

Conversely, when we're riding high and living our very best lives, when we're being the best versions of ourselves that we can possibly be, we must always continue to push ourselves towards more growth and towards *new* levels of goodness. Growth and change are constant. *We shouldn't stop growing when the going gets good.*

Let's go back to the FIGS story for a moment, back to how nurses Trina and Heather put the Ride the Wave principle into action as they were growing their medical apparel business at a meteoric rate.

Even though they were riding high with record sales, they *continued to* improve the design and functionality of their medical scrubs. They came out with new colors and styles; they continued to lock in new manufacturing and distribution deals; they even created a new anti-microbial fabric for their apparel—and these continuous improvements allowed them to ride their wave with ever greater intention and, yes, with greater *grace.*

Even though they were already experiencing extraordinary success, they kept pushing harder and higher, towards the goal of creating the most comfortable and practical medical apparel that had even been created—and in doing so, they changed the face of the entire industry. They knew what their goal was, they remained true to the vision and to their shared beliefs, and as a result, good things happened.

The lesson here is this: the more you are able to fill yourself up with the things that anchor you—the more closely and constantly you align yourself with the essential beliefs, values, and vision that stand at your solid center—the better able you will be to ride that wave.

Similarly—and we all know this is true, because we've all been stuck in places that don't feel quite as comfortable as riding the high waves of contentment and prosperity—it takes extraordinary effort to move from stuck to unstoppable when you're in the throes of crisis and confusion. My point here is that wherever you are in life, whether you're riding high or whether you're struggling to regain your balance after being knocked off your surfboard, *practice continuous growth continuously*. At every stage of life, and in the midst of every layer of life, you must exert a consistent effort to evolve, to improve, and to grow—whether you're riding high or struggling to stay afloat.

The key is awareness. The key is resilience. The key is creating and nurturing the willingness to do the work, to push to new heights, and to learn to navigate the waves of life, because those waves will never cease in their movement. Jon Kabat-Zinn, a noted authority on mindful awareness, said it best: "You can't stop the waves . . . but you can learn to surf."

So, let's end this visualization exercise precisely where we began . . . except at a more elevated level of consciousness. We stand at a heightened state of awareness and a deeper state of gratitude, not just for the lives we lead as leaders and humans, but for the actions we've taken and the conscious choices we've made to bring us to this point.

But what now? Where do we go from here? How do we continue riding this wave? We search for new waves (and new ways!) of growth, and we dig deeper into our stuck-to-unstoppable toolbox so that we can deepen and hone our skills with determination, with grit, and with grace. We begin to adapt (and adopt) these stuck-to-unstoppable principles in our own lives in a way that feels most authentic, most comfortable to us. We refuse to rest on our laurels. So when we *do* fall into the water, we have the flotation devices we need (the stuck-to-unstoppable principles!) to right ourselves and continue moving forward. We crawl back up, we get back on.

And we keep on surfing.

## On Synchrony and Scalability

When we look at how best to ride our waves, and at how best to ensure and maximize the positive momentum we're creating in our lives and in the lives of those around us, it's important to look at all of these efforts *holistically*.

This requires us to look at our efforts as a *collection of continued efforts*, as a series of sustained and synchronous acts that we can control, direct, and manage at all times. This is what will help create a sense of synchrony in our life.

How we view these ongoing efforts—which lenses we decide to use—is vital.

My suggestion is this: learn to look at the world and your place within it not through blinders (because blinders only narrow our vision and limit our capacity to see the wider world around us) but through a *kaleidoscope*, where a countless number of vibrant, brightly colored fragments all fall together to make a single, constantly changing design!

It is this synchrony, this continuous, harmonious movement, that will allow you to maintain your momentum—momentum you will *need*, I should add, when the tides turn and it begins to feel like you're swimming through cement.

This synchrony does not come naturally. It does not occur by osmosis, by accident, or by spontaneous combustion. It requires effort, intention, and conscious choice.

In my own life, the choices I make and the intentions I set for myself are constant. When I awaken each morning, I make the conscious effort and the deliberate choice to create around me the kind of energy I'd like to generate throughout the day. I try to push myself to do better, to stay aware, and to stay in close, conscious contact with the values and beliefs that drive me—and to avoid the things that might distract me or knock me off my center.

This means waking to each new day by taking a few, deep, cleansing breaths, rather than immediately reaching for my phone or signing onto any social media platforms—at least not before I've had a chance to center myself *first*.

I try to move throughout the remainder of the day with this same kind of careful (and joyous!) intentionality. No, it doesn't *always* work (I've never liked the words "always" and "never" because they create an uncomfortable sense of rigidity and inflexibility, neither of which are conducive to growth), but I do my very best, which is all that any of us can do.

The point is that I put in the work, I make the effort, and I hold myself to a certain expectation. Do I hit the mark each and every time? Of course not! I'm human! . . . But at least I know the mark *exists*!

I don't want this to sound too ephemeral, though—I don't want this stuck-to-unstoppable principle to get too bogged down in stardust and gossamer wings . . . because this stuff is real. It is not only useful but applicable in my daily life. It is a tangible tool that enhances my ability to lead and strengthens my driving desire to live with as much authenticity, purpose, and passion as I possibly can. It can work in your life, too.

What comes along with these patterns of purposeful intention, of course, is the recognition that if you continue to have this deliberate approach to your days, these meaningful minutes will eventually turn into meaningful hours, and the hours will turn into weeks, then months, then years, and before you know it, this is how you are living your entire life! There is a beautiful scalability to this concept; the minutes become hours and the hours become your life.

This concept of scalability can work both ways, though, as does everything else in life; everything has its own corresponding polar opposite. Every positive force has a negative force that helps define it. By that I mean this: the dynamics of scalability can work both ways—they can work for you or they can work against you. It takes awareness and conscious choice to help keep the direction and momentum of this scalability concept moving in a positive direction. I'll tell you what I mean.

Some time back, a friend of mine found himself enjoying the tremendous growth and success of his new company. With an annual revenue of about $1.5 million, he was definitely "riding his wave."

But I began to notice a pattern—and as a leader in the space of organizational change, I am proficient and highly trained at recognizing patterns. It is what I *do*. Here's the pattern I was noticing: often, when we would be enjoying a pleasant and relaxing lunch together, for instance, he'd suddenly and without the slightest warning need to cut the lunch short. A FedEx package needed to be sent. Or a document needed to be delivered to a new client.

What was happening was that his life was being constantly interrupted, continually *disrupted*, by the ever-demanding call of business. I want to make it clear here that I am not saying, even for a moment, that these demands, these calls, and these required responses were unimportant. They certainly *were* important, and necessary, if he wanted to continue to grow his business, which he certainly did. But as an organizational change expert (and as his friend) the question I asked him to ask of himself was, "Is this really the most efficient use of my time?" I was beginning to have my doubts.

So we sat down and talked it through. I presented reflective questions to him, which he could ask of himself. I didn't ask the questions. It was important that *he* do that—a perfect example of how self-assessment and reflection, which we explored earlier, can help move us from stuck to unstoppable. The questions sounded something like this:

*How many hours a day do I spend running to FedEx and waiting in line at the post office to mail off a contract? How many minutes of every hour do I spend returning calls? Creating invoices? Hounding clients who are behind in their payments? How do these minutes translate into hours? How do the hours translate into weeks? Weeks into months?*

The point of this scalability exercise was to help him assess the overall utility and efficiency of his actions and to hopefully bring him to this conclusion: If he took all of those minutes, all of those hours, all of those weeks and months and reallocated them instead towards generating new clients, bringing in more business, conducting more strategically focused meetings, how much more revenue would he be able to generate? If he hired an assistant or a business manager to take care of the "busywork" of the business, how much more time would this give him to expand, explore, and discover new levels of growth?

He asked those questions of himself, and the answers that came back were the answers that allowed him to ride his wave to even higher heights. He became more aware of and more discriminating about how he spent his time. He hired an assistant, reallocated his time, and scaled his behavior. He added up all the hours he was spending running here and there, putting out this fire, sending that package, answering that call—and as a result of not only his enhanced awareness but his conscious decision to make different choices and his willingness to actually scale his behavior . . . things changed.

Boy, did they ever change.

In less than two years, *he'd tripled his revenue*. In two years, his revenue climbed from about $1.5 million per year to about $4.5–5 million. Sure, he was riding the wave, even when he was making $1.5 million a year . . . but somehow, the waves kept washing over him in a way that was preventing his continued growth! This scalability model ended up opening his eyes in a way that allowed him to soar to even higher heights.

Are there ways you can begin to measure and scale your own efforts in a similar fashion? Is there a wider vision you can attain that allows you to look at your life from a more expansive, more holistic perspective? Is scalability and synchrony something you are thirsty for in your life? What steps can you take that will allow you to look at your life as a leader and as a human to achieve an even *better* view?

I know one step that you can take immediately: remove the blinders you are wearing. Take them off and keep them off.

Reach for your kaleidoscope instead.

―――――――――

I'll use another example to illustrate the importance of scalability, this time rooted in my own experience.

I caught a really bad case of the flu and struggled with it for thirty-three days. Fortunately, it was not a severe case. Hospitalization was not necessary, nor did I suffer from any major, debilitating symptoms . . . but it did have a deleterious effect on my overall countenance. It interrupted the rigor and rhythm of my daily life. It created waves that were a little higher than normal. The waters around me were definitely swirling and churning with more furious force.

I stopped exercising with any regularity. I stopped writing in my journal (which I normally do on a daily basis). I stopped hiking (again, a regular activity), rolled up my yoga mat and tossed it into the corner, and spent more time on the sofa than I probably had since I binge-watched *Game of Thrones*!

But here's where the scalability model comes into beautiful play: I could *see and feel* that the scales of my energy and efficiency had taken a downward turn. Because of my heightened awareness and my ability to self-assess, I understood that I was moving in a downward spiral rather than an upward spiral.

It was this awareness, this ability to see (and therefore scale) my behavior, that nudged me gently back on track. All of this inaction was simply no longer an option. I visualized what would happen if those thirty-three days I was out of commission turned into thirty-three months, and those months turned into . . . well, you get the idea. I ran the mental numbers, adjusted the mental scale, recalibrated those numbers in a way that shifted my momentum from on-the-couch weary to let-me-get-up-and-get-moving energy, and as a result, things began to change. Slowly but surely, I began to push myself back into action.

Whether you scale up or scale down is totally up to you. The beauty of scalability is that it can be adjusted in either direction, depending on the situation you're facing and the conscious choices you choose to make. What's important is that you are able to see beyond where you are and get a view of a better place, a more optimal space, with a more positive outcome.

Are you willing to teach the people around you how to adjust, refit, and recalibrate their scales in a way that brings them the most benefit and the greatest growth? Can you *teach* this skill to others so that they too can learn to push themselves from stuck to unstoppable if they hit a snag or stumble and fall? How can you breathe life into this scalability model so that it can be employed and applied by those who surround you?

Give careful thought to these questions. Then give equally careful thought to the answers.

Then . . . make it happen.

––––––––––

## A Global Embrace

It takes energy, effort, and incredible balance—physical, mental, emotional, and spiritual balance—to ride the wave successfully. We will fall off occasionally; we are human, not super-human. We also, all of us, exist in this ocean of life *together*. No matter how successful, how prosperous, or how financially savvy you are, the fact of the matter is that none of us ride this wave alone. It is vital to remember this.

There are people around us who help us remain afloat—whether it's our customers, clients, distributors, employees, or the people who work so hard to clean our offices at the end of each and every day—and it is this tribe of trusted humans, some of whom we know well and some we've never even met, who help ensure our buoyancy and balance. We navigate these waters with other people.

It is this sense of connectivity to others, this sense of collective belonging, that anchors us and helps keep us grounded. As leaders, we must remain constantly aware of these connections and eternally vigilant about doing all we can to keep these connections strong, vibrant, and alive.

We are not islands unto ourselves; we *belong* to each other. As we continue to explore the upper rooms of this literary home of ours, try to keep this notion of *collective buoyancy* at the forefront of your mind. As leaders, it is our awesome, somber, and joyous obligation. This is higher-order thinking.

On an equally expansive scale, particularly when we talk about the importance of this notion of collective buoyancy, let's remember that when you benefit or when I benefit, we *all* benefit. When your new employee masters a new skill or develops a new set of tools that will help him deliver his product more efficiently, the entire organization benefits. This kind of scalability is *infinite*; it keeps going and going and going. I am reminded of a popular, powerful quote that perfectly captures this sentiment: "We rise by lifting others."

In a very real sense, this kind of positive, forward-moving momentum extends far beyond the businesses we lead and the organizations we manage. It extends into our communities, our neighborhoods, and eventually it will flow into the larger world around us. The flow is continuous . . . and *we* are responsible for its continuous momentum.

This means that the good we create—whether it unfolds in our organization, in our homes, or in our communities—can trickle up (and trickle down, I suppose) to the wider world around us. This is when goodness evolves on a global scale. This is goodness that lives within each of us and all of us.

To think that we have a direct hand in its creation is mind-blowing, isn't it? Not just an idle hand, either, but a purposeful, powerful hand that creates momentum and moves the needle in a positive direction.

That's not just riding the wave. It's us—*all* of us—helping to make the world around us a better, happier, more harmonious place.

We must begin now.

## *Chapter Eight*
# KEEP ON KEEPING ON

THINK BACK TO THE WAVES WE WERE RIDING IN THE LAST CHAPTER.
You will remember that we identified ways to continue riding these waves to even higher heights, to keep pushing up, up, up on whatever given path we have chosen for ourselves in a way that ensures our continued growth and consistent improvement.

In this chapter, we'll dig deeper into this practice and principle of not just maintaining our momentum, but growing it, day by day, moment by moment, second by second. As we enter into this upper-level room of our literary home, we'll ascend to an even higher level of thinking, being, doing . . . and becoming.

It's the *becoming* part that I want us to inhabit here.

> To evolve into what you have not yet become requires emotional maturity and spiritual intelligence. Your mindset and thought patterns are central.

We have arrived, finally, at a point in our stuck-to-unstoppable journey where we can focus almost exclusively on the inner work that is involved in moving forward, in leading a life of balance and connection, in aligning everything around us in a way that is holistic and harmonious. Now we are prepared, because we have accumulated the necessary tools and the knowledge from previous chapters, to focus exclusively on the mental work that's involved in this journey. Think of it as inner work from our upper room. This is higher-order thinking, indeed.

We couldn't have explored this facet of thought in earlier chapters simply because we weren't really working from that multi-layered base of understanding just yet. You don't know what you know until you know it, right?

But the beauty of these scaffolded chapters, as I've explained before, is that they build upon one another. Like the real-life scaffolds we see on construction sites, these scaffolded chapters actually *carry us* from one level of understanding to another. They create solid planks—platforms—from which we can ascend from one level to the next.

Now that we have arrived at the very highest level of our literary home (visualize us, now, either standing in the attic . . . or maybe even on the roof!) we can view all that we have learned from a more fully integrated, aerial perspective.

And the view is absolutely breathtaking.

————

## The Giant Sequoia

In a very real way, this chapter leads us right back to where we began, back to a vital, foundational concept that we explored at the beginning of the book: awareness.

But now, we can look at the importance of developing a heightened sense of awareness from a far deeper (and wider) perspective. If we are to lead our organizations and the people who make up our organizations as effectively, as efficiently, and—I use this next word with intention and purpose—as *lovingly* as possible, it will require us to tap into and develop an emotional, mental, and even spiritual clarity that comes from within. This is an inside job.

For us to "keep on keeping on"—and for us to guide, grow, and inspire the people around us so that they too can keep on keeping on, we must turn inward first. Into ourselves. This inward turn is mandatory before the outward turn towards others can be impactful, meaningful, and fully authentic.

> I need to say this again: *our mindset matters.* Being able to understand our inner motives and true aspirations is the only way we will grow, and the only way we will help others grow. This is not easy work; it takes effort, intention, desire, and, ultimately, action.

It requires us to design, develop, and sometimes even de-tangle our own set of values and beliefs, and to ask ourselves some essential questions that only we ourselves can answer. No one else can answer these deeply personal and introspective questions for us *but* us:

- *Do I know what drives me?*

- *Are the various aspects of my life fully aligned and balanced in a way that allows them to comfortably coexist, deep down at my inner core?*

- *Am I spending enough time with myself to know where I actually belong?*

- *Am I thinking at deeper levels about my ultimate purpose and passion in life?*

- *Am I paying attention to the forces that compel me, or am I allowing myself to remain stuck in circular ruts and negative interactions that move me nowhere?*

- *When I look inside myself, what is it that I actually see?*

It's ironic, in a way, that this elevated form of thought—inner thought and evaluative reflection—is also the most elemental, the most foundational. Getting *up here* requires that we begin, first, at the lowest level of scaffolding—at that all-important principle of awareness. It starts with awareness, and builds up, up, up from there—just like the chapters and flow of this book and the sequence and order of these principles. This is mental scaffolding at its best and most beautiful.

So we return, full circle, to where we began—except this time we stand in a deeper, more fully saturated state of understanding and awareness. As we stand on the roof of our literary home right now, we understand that awareness, at every level and in every circumstance, is what will allow us to push forward from stuck to unstoppable.

What we have now is a more full-bodied awareness, far more

robust and rounded out than when we opened the first pages of this book. What we have now, as we have studied, reflected, evaluated, and celebrated these stuck-to-unstoppable concepts, is, well, *a shining awareness of awareness*!

We know now that if we are to live lives of passion and purpose, if we are to lead and inspire others in a way that ensures their continued growth and development, and if we are to continually push ourselves to higher heights—to keep on keeping on in every conceivable form and fashion—then our *inner equilibrium* must be as stabilizing and as deeply rooted as the great sequoia in a redwood forest.

As we reflect on what it actually *looks* like to keep on keeping on, and on what it *feels* like to persist and persevere no matter the setback or the circumstance, we must also reflect on the inner machine that drives us forward, because it will be these inner places that give us the propulsive energy we'll need to continue generating our momentum. To keep on keeping on.

Again, I don't want these words and concepts to feel mystical and amorphous. These concepts are not cloud-based. They are firmly grounded and deeply rooted in real-world sensibilities (the sequoia tree again).

Your ability to understand your essential self is as real as the hand in front of your face. In fact, let's digress for a moment to perform a simple "rooted-in-reality" exercise: I want you to actually hold your hand up in front of your face for a moment. Go ahead, do it. Hold up your hand and maybe even wave it around in front of you . . . just so you can be aware of its visual and physical reality! In the midst of your own movement will come the awareness, again, that conscious choice and deliberate action really do belong to you. You made the decision to hold up your hand, which led to the action itself. This simple act will, in turn, lead us to the ultimate affirmation that we hold within ourselves the ability to decide . . . and the ability to take action. Through the lifting of one's hand, then, the concept of conscious choice is brought to life.

What we have explored and discovered together, as we've moved from room to room in this literary home of ours, are concepts that are at once infinite and finite—and how you decide to weave the threads of these concepts into your own human experience is entirely up to you. This is your journey. These threads belong to you and you alone.

You will know best how to customize and crystallize these concepts in a way that makes the most sense in your own life. I will not know. Your neighbor will not know. Not even your best friend or your boss will know how best to incorporate these principles into your human experience. You will know. Isn't that another wonderful reason to make sure that the path to your inner self is clearly marked and free of obstructions?

Know thyself!

Think of the great sequoia again, deeply rooted and solidly connected to the earth. As ancient as time itself.

————

Let's dig deeper into this notion that for us to continue striving, growing, reaching, and evolving, we must be aware of what moves us from the inside out.

> Look, listen: Before you can lead others in a way that is authentic and complete, you must first move from a place of inner understanding and acceptance. Stay true to that, and you stay true to the people around you.

Let what drives you internally be the compass you rely on to drive others externally. Without that internal navigation system, you are lost. *Depend* on it. Let it lead you so that you can, in turn, lead others. Then and only then can you teach others to rely on their own inner compasses with equal intensity. Remember: you cannot teach what you do not know.

Teach your people to tap into those places where their deepest selves reside. These are often hidden places, difficult to find. You must help shine the light for them so that they can find them. It is up to them to find. It is up to you to shine the light so that they can clearly see. *This* is the mark of true—and great—leadership.

I will use an example from my own life experience.

After receiving a promotion to a very senior position, the CEO said to me, "I do not want you to become a textbook picture of an executive. You received this promotion not just because of your level of experience and expertise, but because of *who you are deep down inside*. You must continue being exactly who you are. I do not need you becoming anyone else."

I remember sighing—literally sighing—in amazement and with great gratitude, then saying to him, "I will do exactly that.

I will always remain connected to, and centered within, exactly who I am."

For two executives to be communicating with each other in these terms, using verbiage like this, is proof positive these concepts are not rooted in fantasy or sprinkled with stardust. They are real, and what's more, when we ascribe to these principles, when we place value upon them, we bring bottom-line, real-world benefits to our organizations as well. This isn't just good human interaction. It's good business.

## The Awareness of Awareness

There's a model that was originally developed in the change management space during a time when the discipline itself was just beginning to evolve. It has quickly gained popularity and is used quite widely now across multiple industries and spaces, because of its universal applicability. Created in the 1990s by former Bell Labs engineer and entrepreneur Jeff Hiatt and published in a white paper titled "The Perfect Change," the ADKAR Model is an outcome-oriented change management method that aims to limit resistance to organizational change. This model helps us initiate and embrace change in our organizations, a useful tool given that we all know how challenging change can be.

As you look at ways to lead your employees and your organization to higher forms of being and becoming, you'll quickly realize that change is necessary. Perhaps not major change. Maybe just an organizational tweak here or a values-and-vision-based tweak there. But because we all know that change itself is the only constant—not just in business but in life itself—these tools might be helpful to you in your own journey:

## The ADKAR Model of Change Management

- *Awareness:* The awareness of the need for change.
- *Desire:* The desire to participate and support the change.
- *Knowledge:* The knowledge of how to change.
- *Ability:* The ability to implement the desired skills and behavior.
- *Reinforcement:* How to sustain the change.

The wonderful thing about this model is that it can be used in virtually any aspect of life. It helps us look at change through a wider lens.

Perhaps consider trying it within your own sphere of influence!

## Our Unique Lives

I like to remind myself that I am beautifully human. I am beautifully flawed, ever evolving, and continuously unfolding. It is time, now, for you to embrace this same understanding of yourself.

You, too, are uniquely, beautifully human; you are multi-layered and intricately hewn. No two of us are alike. No two leaders are alike. No two employees are alike. Count this as a good thing, simply because it is a crystal-clear reflection of the human race itself. We are as diverse and as different from one another as the colors of a rainbow, as different and distinct as the brightly colored fragments of that kaleidoscope through which we learned to view the world around us in the previous chapter.

> As leaders, this is what we want to instill in our employees too. We must teach them to lean into both their strengths and their weaknesses, to accept them all.

In fact, the very act of leaning into our weaknesses allows us to address those weaknesses and transform them into strengths (or at the very least, to avoid letting those weaknesses create disruptive or consistently negative patterns in our lives and in our organizations).

This is where the inner work becomes important—as well as the need to understand how this inner work supports, reflects, and complements the outer work we perform as leaders. For us to truly reflect the values and the vision of the companies we work for, or the businesses we run, or the family units of which we are part, we must first understand the values and vision that move within us, from the inside out—because it starts on the inside and works its way out. This fundamental understanding of ourselves is what will actually allow us to drive our *companies* forward! The direct correlation exists.

We are all on different journeys. My journey is different than yours; I face an entirely different set of circumstances than you, and you face an entirely different set of circumstances that the co-worker down the hall or the CEO in the corner office. What binds us together—and what drives us forward in a way that allows us to keep on keeping on, in synchronized lockstep—is a healthy, holistically based appreciation of our differences, and an acceptance of the fact that even as individuals with varying beliefs, we come together in an organization to reflect the organization's larger beliefs, values, and goals. Both can exist simultaneously.

The leader who creates an organizational culture that respects, nurtures, and encourages each employee for the person that they are is the leader who believes that each of us can soar to higher heights . . . which enables our organizations to soar to even higher heights as well. Again, there is a direct correlation.

So as you figure out how best to weave the threads of these stuck-to-unstoppable principles into a single, beautiful tapestry, remember (once again) that you know yourself best. Heck, you know yourself better than *anybody*—which means that you are the architect of your own "home," the narrator of your own story.

It's also important to keep in mind, from a change management perspective, that developing different ways of doing things—change itself—can be highly stressful and unsettling. If you're a leader, you already know this. This is when our ability to turn inward and draw strength from the emotional compass that exists within us proves to be of great comfort and sustenance. This kind of emotional (and yes, spiritual) maturity gives us clarity, courage, and confidence to lead others through change.

Having this "collective guidance system" is particularly important for teams of people who are working towards the same goal. Whether you're a small-business owner with only a few employees or a CEO with thousands of them, sharing the same guidance system will help you achieve your goals and push you through crises with renewed vigor.

---

## Seeing Beyond What You Can See

When we go back to how nurses Trina Spear and Heather Hasson kept on keeping on as they pushed higher and higher, harder and harder, towards their goal of creating the most efficient, comfortable, and stylish medical apparel in the industry, let's remember how they did it. Even at their highest heights, they still recognized each other's unique characteristics and human distinctions—two people with the same goal, the same vision, yet two uniquely human individuals who were ready, willing, and able to elevate themselves beyond their differences to realize a common, singular vision.

Of course, even at those heights, they had good days . . . and not-so-good days. That's what life is about, right? It is far from easy, and we all know how external forces can occasionally knock us off-track (or off that surfboard) at any moment. But Trina and Heather already had their flotation devices at hand. As the waves of their growing company ebbed and flowed around them, they *took care of each other* and held on tight to the common, unwavering believe in their vision. This shared inner belief and common inner understanding was their flotation device!

> This is what you should try to do as a leader as well: try to align yourself, first, with your inner vision, with your internal guidance system.

From that will flow an ability to align and connect with a larger, more expansive, collective vision—your organization's vision, your family's vision, your community's vision, the list goes on and on—and from there you'll be capable of aligning with a vision that brings benefit to the larger world around you in the most expansive embrace of all! This, again, is higher-order thinking.

From this elevated rooftop view of our literary home we can see more, do more, and become more. Everything is open to us now, in a way that it simply wasn't open to us back when our journey first began, when we were taking those first tentative steps through the front door. The rooftop view opens up more expansive ways to look at both life and leadership. It allows us to look at organizational change itself, for instance, through a more expansive lens—through that brilliant kaleidoscope, rather than those the narrowly focused blinders.

Here's an example of how this elevated view can also expand and elevate our overall philosophical approach to leadership and organizational change. When you can see things from a higher view, from a more elevated perspective, it has an effect on your *decision-making*, on the conscious choices you make and the behaviors you display as a leader.

It allows you to look at things from different vantage

points—vantage points on decisions you might not personally agree with or subscribe to, but which you embrace and support anyway because you're able to recognize that they will ultimately bring the greatest good.

Consider this example:

Some time ago, after a somewhat emotionally charged meeting of senior leaders who were discussing the possibility of making a major change that would end up pushing the company in a new direction, one of the managers came to me and shared something that was at once inspiring and visionary.

"I disagree with the decision that was made at the executive level," they said. "But I'm going to stay quiet about it because I cannot see what they see."

I want to repeat that sentence again because it's such a beautiful representation of the rooftop perspective we've been exploring in this chapter, this elevated, emotionally mature thinking:

"I cannot see what they see."

What that told me was that the employee was open enough to trust others, to place full confidence in the senior leaders who were tasked with evaluating and implementing the change, and because this employee had a clear understanding of (and a close alignment with) the organization's vision, he was able to put personal beliefs aside for the greater good of the organization.

This employee refused to let their ego win. Personal disagreements were not allowed to upset or obstruct the larger balance and the collective equilibrium. Cohesion was achieved . . . and this took considerable inner work. It required an aerial view. It required, above all, trust in a larger vision and a greater good—as well as trust in the leaders who were tasked with steering their organization *towards* that greater good. This employee leaned into the notion of "seeing beyond what they could see."

Are you teaching your employees to see beyond what they can see? This is called trust . . . and until we learn to trust ourselves, we will not be able to trust one another.

Internal work has profound external implications.

———————

I've worked with employees from all over the world—thousands of people across the globe—and they know that I trust them, instinctively, to do their jobs and to do their jobs well. Regardless of what industry I was working in or what specific role I played throughout my career, I encouraged whatever team I was leading to "run your area of business like you own it." I place my full trust and my full confidence in them to take similar ownership and accountability with the employees who work for them as well; it's a ripple effect. It is important that I empower them and afford them full autonomy to perform their duties in the best way they know how. The need for me to micro-manage seldom arises.

There are *boundaries*, of course, within which they know they have to remain—we are a well-run organization, after all— but there is a trust between us that is born of self-confidence, awareness, and emotional intelligence. Again, this is internal work that has profound external implications and impact.

> As a leader, you must know this: you can run the numbers and produce the financial statements and expand the profit margins until the cows come home . . . but in the end (and, I suppose, in the beginning, too) it all boils down to how you treat your employees.

Do you value them? Do you create a culture of trust and mutual respect? Do you empower them to be the very best versions of themselves that they can possibly be? Have you taught them to see beyond that which they can see?

When your answers come back "yes" to *all* of the questions I just asked, then you've set yourself on track towards not just excellent employee relations but good, strong business strategy as well—because when your employees feel seen and heard, as we've discussed before, this translates into a better, healthier, more productive customer experience . . . which helps the financials fall into place. Again, the correlation is direct and specific.

When we talk about empowering (and enabling) our employees to get into the sky and soar to their highest heights—or face the rigors of running a successful company with nary a hiccup, mistake, or misstep—we are giving them a false (and unhealthy) sense of hope. They need to understand that external events will occasionally knock them down. Profits will take a downward turn. New products will launch and fizzle. Lay-offs, cutbacks, and downsizing will come. But when you're consistent about the culture you're creating, you learn to navigate through these things. You learn to push forward and persevere, even when the waves get high.

Make sure you teach your employees this too—the concept stands at the center of their ability and their potential for growth. You want to do all you can to retain your people—particularly those who bring significant value and vision to your organization, and you owe them the sustained effort. (Plus, remember that it's extremely expensive to hire, train, and retrain new employees! Why absorb the additional significant expense if it can be avoided?)

As you find your footing on this rooftop, and as you become more comfortable and confident with this aerial view, remember again that the capacity to think these higher-order thoughts already exists within you! This is a fast-moving river that is already running within. All you have to do is tap into it. Dip your toe into the water. Drop your hand into its beautiful depths. Train your brain to think more expansively. Again, I don't want to make this sound easy—there is significant and sustained effort involved, no two ways about it—but this river belongs to you. To navigate these new waters, understand that you already have the flotation devices you need to remain buoyant. They're deep, deep inside of you, waiting to be discovered.

Everything you need is everything you already have.

All you really need to do is turn inward and reach in.

## *Chapter Nine*
# THE ULTIMATE ENDGAME

READ THIS CHAPTER TITLE AGAIN.

Now go ahead and put this title into the form of a question so that you're asking yourself what I consider to be the most essential question of all:

*What is your ultimate endgame?*

Why do you do the things you do? What moves you? Motivates you? Wakes you up in the morning? You will remember in the previous chapter we talked about the vital importance of getting (and staying) in touch with our inner guidance system as the surest, most authentic way to keep on keeping on, whether keeping on means continuing to ride a wave or struggling to regain our balance.

We talked about the importance of taking the inward pivot *first*—and how that inward pivot allows us to take the outward pivot—towards our families, our jobs, our communities, and the whole, wide, beautiful world around us. And we talked about doing it with clarity, confidence, and conviction, right?

Now, as we reach the point where we're trying to identify our ultimate endgame, we need to drill down a little deeper into this concept and ask ourselves this question:

*Now that we've turned inward . . . what do we see?
What's in there?*

---

## Your Purpose and Your Passion

Again, let's use Trina and Heather's meteoric rise to success in the medical apparel industry to help us answer these questions.

It's clear that Trina and Heather had strong inner compasses. They knew how to navigate themselves towards (and remain firmly rooted in) their inner center. But they also went a step further: once they were in that inner space, there was no confusion about what they saw. Their collective vision—their ultimate endgame—was as clear as a bell. Put simply, their purpose and their passion never varied, flip-flopped, or fluctuated. They wanted to bring a more practical, more aesthetically pleasing version of medical scrubs to the marketplace, which is precisely what they did.

From the very beginning—even when their dream was more of an amorphous *idea*—Trina and Heather were vitally aware of their passion and their purpose. No, they weren't celebrities or social media influencers or TikTok sensations with millions of viewers and countless followers. They were nurses with an idea and a vision, and they were confident that this vision of theirs would bring value to the world around them. This "inner vision" was even clearer because they had a deep and intimate understanding of the product they were going to create, and for what reason. They were also peers with the potential customers they would one day serve, with the fellow nurses who surrounded them, supported them, provided constant feedback, tested out the prototypes, and who knew from experience (and also from their own deep-down places of authentic truth) what was necessary to hone this product in a way that would bring the most benefit.

As a result of all of this, Trina and Heather didn't just bring a new product onto the market. *They disrupted the space around them.*

They reinvented and redefined the entire market. Through hard work, inner vision, and a crystal-clear understanding of their ultimate endgame, they *compelled* themselves to be unstoppable in their goals. And after six years of conceptualizing, honing, visualizing, improving, listening, and remaining closely, unswervingly aligned with their ultimate endgame, the company went public and opened on the New York Stock Exchange valued at more than $6 billion.

They started with an inward turn, staying true to their passion and their purpose, which made the *outward* turn all the more rewarding.

Fortunately, "reward" can come in many different forms.

---

## There Can Be a Multitude of Endgames!

This much is clear: Trina and Heather's relentlessly laser-like focus on their endgame eventually guided them towards extreme wealth and extraordinary financial success. And while financial gain and healthy profit margins can be (and usually are) mighty motivators, this doesn't have to be the *only* motivator or the single, solitary endgame. There can be a healthy multitude of endgames that co-exist and live comfortably together, all wrapped up in single, beautifully layered vision!

As a businesswoman myself, I will be the first to acknowledge that profit and money-making motivate . . . but even the *pursuit* of profit allows us to turn inward, yet again, to ask ourselves an essential question:

> *Is profit-making my only endgame, or are there a healthy multitude of endgames that can co-exist in this space?*

There is nothing wrong with wanting to build a multi-billion-dollar business. The desire itself is bold, brave, and refreshingly audacious. It is entirely possible to have a healthy, holistic relationship with money *and* with the process of pursuing it. But when you turn inward to find the touchstone that grounds you, the inner compass that guides you, and the internal roadmap that leads you, try to make sure those tools help you create a clear vision as you move forward. Try to create and nurture a vision within you that—and here I come back to a word I used a few sentences earlier—can be *holistically* applied.

If that billion-dollar company (or even a portion of the profits that come from it) helps improve the community in some way, or if some of the profit is designated to flow towards those who are in need or even to the valued employees within it who helped steer it towards success—the concept of profit-sharing at its very best—then these are holistic goals with wide-ranging positive impact. It is not just profit for the sake of profit.

Yet even here, I must be careful: Who am *I* to say that having a profit-only-for-the-sake-of-profit endgame is misguided or incorrect? What we decide to pursue and how we decide to pursue it are decisions that belong to us and us alone. I am not in the business of judging. My point is this: when you *do* turn inward to find that touchstone, to rely on that inner compass to guide you and that roadmap to lead you, make sure you are comfortable with the direction that it takes you. Give thought to your motive; try to make sure you are creating good in the world along with that profit. The two are not mutually exclusive, after all.

> Similarly, as a leader in whatever industry space you happen to stand in, always try to give other people the space they deserve to stand along with you.

If it's your employees, boost them up. Develop them for growth. Align them for success. As we've already discovered in previous chapters, when your people feel valued, heard, seen, and confident that they are a vital part of your ultimate vision, good things happen.

Positive energy begets positive energy. These are the very people you have empowered to help move your company forward; these are the very people who will help grow your company's profit margins and who are out there, every day, nurturing healthy relationships with your customers and your client base! They deserve to stand in this inner vision space too.

You stand where you are now, whether you're a business owner or a corporate executive, because the people who surround you helped get you there. Keep them not just in the periphery of your vision as you move forward in your leadership life, but in that quiet, centered, inwardly turned vision as well, in that place where your inner goals and your essential values live.

Keep them clearly in sight—not just in your peripheral vision, and not just when it's convenient or you're feeling particularly benevolent—but *continuously*, because these people are your active agents, your catalysts for growth and change. They provide the impetus and the momentum to help get you where you ultimately need to go.

---

## Say it. Write it. Claim it!

Here's the tricky part of all of this inner mind work—particularly if you happen to be a senior executive or company leader: all this internal messaging and quiet reflection is, by definition, a very *quiet* process!

Since we're talking to ourselves, really, and directing our thinking inward (initially, at least) rather than outward towards other people, we don't always know what decibel level to use!

This next question I pose might sound a little silly, but it is totally legitimate and fully grounded in a real-world sensibility:

> *When we're talking to ourselves, how can we make sure we really hear what we're saying?*

The good news is that there are tools and techniques at our disposal that can help us solidify the internal messages and thoughts we send to ourselves. It takes effort and intention to train our brains to turn inward and speak to the quiet recesses of our minds: they simply didn't *teach* us this stuff in business school. It will require not just training, but *re-training* our brains (and our minds).

Remember that the brain is like a muscle: the more we use it, the stronger and more pliable it becomes. Conversely, if we only "lift and lower" in one direction, we are limiting the brain's flexibility and dexterity. So it stands to reason that if we want to move our minds in a different direction—if we want to expand our thinking and deepen our emotional intelligence—we'll need to use a different set of weights.

In my own life, I have developed many creative tools for this very reason. On a daily (and sometimes even hourly) basis, I rely on these simple tools to help ensure that I can fully hear the stream of positive self-talk and healthy affirmations I'm constantly sending to myself. We live in a noisy, nattering world: it's difficult, sometimes, to cut through the clutter and the static so that we can hear ourselves think . . . and hear ourselves when we *speak* to ourselves!

One of these tools—and you can use this, too—is the sticky note.

Ah, sticky-notes are my dear friends. I use them regularly to direct (and redirect) my thoughts inward, particularly helpful when I'm feeling a little stuck, a little overwhelmed, or a little off-balance.

My mom infused me with many of these sayings and beliefs when I was very young, and they still move and inspire me at very deep and fundamental level. By writing them down on sticky notes, and reading them as I'm brushing my teeth in the morning or taking off my jewelry before bed, I am rewriting the circuitry of my brain and creating space for these positive affirmations.

This is also a bold and beautiful reminder that we do, indeed, have complete control over the thoughts we think and the messages we convey to ourselves. *We get to make this conscious choice.* And by writing these messages down, saying them aloud, and repeating them in our time of need, we're planting seeds of positive energy in our minds . . . energy that will sprout and take hold when we least expect it.

On any given day, here's an example of some of the mental affirmations you might see if you were to step into my home:

## Trish-isms
*"Breathe."*
*"I follow my bliss."*
*"This too shall pass."*
*"Blessings are coming."*
*"The job of giving is the greatest joy of all."*

> "Remember to focus on what's
> in your control."
> "My ability to concentrate improves
> significantly."
> "Relieve yourself of yesterday's burdens
> and bitterness."
> "I am proud of every step I take towards
> reaching my goals."
> "You'll be amazed at what you will
> attract after you start believing in what
> you deserve."

---

## The Mountains before Us

As we visualize, internalize, and affirm our ultimate endgame—
and because we are all on different journeys, with different and
unique sets of challenges—this endgame will vary from person
to person. Let's remember that that the horizon before us is
ever-changing. There will be new mountains to ascend, new
valleys to traverse, and new paths to discover, all waiting for
us far, far off in the distance.

Take a moment to congratulate yourself for making is this
far; for having a sustained and positive impact on your organization and on the humans who live within the spaces of
your organization. But remember your life as a leader is never

really finished; this journey is fluid and ever-evolving. There will always be a new mountain to climb, a new relationship to build, a new client or customer to attract, a new hire to embrace, train, and motivate.

The question becomes, then, a question of how best to deal with this fluidity and constant movement, because it is, itself, intangible. It is not a profit-loss statement. It is not a balance sheet. It is not a long-term strategic plan or a Power Point slide or a brightly colored pie chart on projected market saturation. This is life and these are the intangibilities of life—things we have not been trained to focus upon . . . at least not until now.

Hopefully, this journey we have taken together, exploring the various rooms in our literary home, has opened new doors and windows for you and has given you the tools and techniques you need to continue your journey towards becoming unstoppable. That is my hope and my prayer.

> Your life as a leader, a motivator, a teacher, and as a human being who is responsible for the nourishment and well-being of others (after all, when you sign your name to the front of your employees' paychecks each week, you are accepting responsibility for putting food on their table and bringing sustenance into their homes) should remain in close alignment with your goals and your inner vision.

Make sure your ultimate endgame remains clear, inclusive, and welcoming. When it falls out of line—and it will sometimes, because we are not perfect—you already have the tools you need to get yourself back on track. Use them.

Above all, make sure that when you look inward, the person you see is the most authentic version of yourself that you can possibly be. If tweaks are necessary to get you closer to this ideal version, then let the tweaking begin. None of us are perfect. If bad habits and negative patterns need to be broken, then by all means let the *breaking* begin. You hold the roadmap. Within you lies the power of conscious choice.

Let the question become, in those quiet moments of turning inward:

> *Will today be the day you will give up who you've been to become who you want to be?*

Then let your answer be yes.

"YES!"

Today is the day indeed.

## *Chapter 10*
# THE STUCK-TO-UNSTOPPABLE PLAYBOOK

So here we stand, together.

We have explored each and every room of our literary home. We've stress-tested the foundation. Flung open every door and window. We've even crawled into the narrow, sometimes-uncomfortable crawl spaces and the shadowy, cobwebbed corridors where little light shines.

We need to be as comfortable in these uncomfortable spaces as we are in the bright, sunny rooms. This is what life *brings* us: shadowy corners where we sometimes feel stuck . . . and wonderful, wide-open spaces where the sun streams in, beckoning us towards the light.

No matter which rooms you stand in, or how stuck you might feel, you now possess the tools to help you develop *actionable strategies* to move yourself forward. You now have the awareness. You now have the flotation devices you need to provide buoyancy, and the ballast you need when the waters get rough and the waves threaten to submerge you completely.

I want to return to this very important concept of *actionable strategies* for a moment, because the concept itself is a game-changer: When you are standing at the precipice of change, or perhaps at its solid, sometimes-scary center, or maybe even in its dizzying aftermath, life feels unsettling. Having an actionable strategy close at hand to help you navigate through these swirling waters is not only comforting, it is efficient. It is wise. It is intelligent. It is pro-active.

And it is the most responsible way to lead and live.

Whether you're leading your company through major organizational realignment or facing the winds of change in your own personal life (and I should also add that change doesn't always have to be earth-shattering; change at *any* level, in *any* capacity, can carry within it potentially destabilizing energy!) it is entirely possible for you to remain in forward-moving motion. Put simply: we all get stuck, but *being* stuck doesn't mean *staying* stuck.

Not anymore, anyway.

You now have access to the principles within this Stuck-to-Unstoppable Playbook, which makes you the head coach in the game . . . the head coach in *your* game. The field belongs to you. Your players are waiting. The clock on the scoreboard is ticking. The crowd is excited and expectant. The stadium is packed. As head coach, the next steps are up to you.

So snap open your playbook and call this beautiful, ever-changing game of living and leading into action! And proceed with the vital awareness that this time around, as the plays commence, they will commence on your terms. You design them. You possess the knowledge and the tools. The field is yours.

What makes this playbook so powerful and so relevant is its unique customizability. These principles come from me, but I've given them to you as a gift—and now they are waiting to be carefully fitted into the various folds and layers of your life in a way that only you know best. In fact, this customizability is what I appreciate most about these principles—and over time, the more and more you weave these threads into the fabric of your life experience, my guess is that this is what you will appreciate about these principles, too: their human contour and their miraculous malleability.

Mold these principles into the contours of your life in a way that creates the most comfortable fit. You are the sculptor. You hold the clay.

------

## The Gift of a Lifetime

I have gifted these principles to you with what I hope has been humility and grace. These are principles and practices that I have developed, honed, and sharpened over the course of an entire lifetime—and they become yours now because we have traveled this journey together. The transfer, then, has been made: I have shared this playbook with a sense of purpose, a sense of passion, and yes, I have shared these stuck-to-unstoppable principles with love.

Leaders love too.

> The fact that we are humans first and leaders second is a fact that should be celebrated, not shirked. We are complicated, multi-layered beings, which means we get stuck sometimes, even at the highest levels. Being stuck is a part of life; it's the staying stuck that is optional. *Choose to not stay stuck.*

Our goal is certainly not to avoid these feelings of paralysis—indeed, being able to lean into them and even honor the discomfort we might be feeling *as we're feeling it* shows a heightened and necessary sense of awareness—and it is this awareness that will help propel us forward. So in a very real sense, the challenges and unexpected changes we face in our lives are what actually help us grow. They are what strengthen us and they are what connect us to and stabilize us at our very center . . . if we employ the tools at our disposal to help us in this effort. It all boils down to conscious choice.

Conscious choice, too, is the gift of a lifetime. Use it. Activate it. Awaken it in your own life. Use the playbook you are holding in your hands right now to help get you there. Accept this gift from me, because I offer it to you with full-bodied grace, deep gratitude, and every good intention.

This is what I *do*! I teach humans to become *consistently unstoppable*. I guide them through the stuck points, towards the waters of growth and the waters of resilience, flexibility, tenacity, good-old-fashioned grit, and, ultimately, towards the willingness to change. We stand now at a place where all of these rivers and waterways converge.

And now you must float.

———————

## From Negative to Positive

In each and every chapter, you'll remember that we somehow always swung back to the importance of awareness. Awareness is where it all begins. Without it, we have no compass. No playbook. No inner guidance system. With it, the world opens up to us in infinite and unimaginable ways. In everything you do as you move forward, try to keep your own awareness at your steady center. Nurture it and grow it, for it can always be nurtured, grown, and lifted to new levels. Awareness, like change, is fluid and in constant motion. It can always find new ways to express itself, new ways to unfold. Remember the lotus blossom.

Your own awareness, in fact, will be what helps push you past the negative self-talk and the dark, downwardly turned spirals you will inevitably encounter as you move through life and navigate change. Mindset matters.

You now hold the tools to manage and move your mindset from negative to positive. You—and only you—hold the power and the potential to redefine the way you view yourself.

Remember that "Uns" list we examined back in Chapter Three? The list with the positive "Uns" and the negative "Uns"? When you're feeling stuck, no longer will you need to pull from the negative side of that list, from descriptors like "Unstable," "Unwilling," and "Unpleasant."

No!

Now you have the resources to change your own narrative. To flip the script. To redefine this list and *push yourself past stuck*, to a place where forward-moving motion and conscious choice live and breathe. To a place where new descriptors live, like "Unflappable," "Unbent," "Unapologetic," and the most important descriptor of all?

"UNSTOPPABLE."

What is the next thing you will do in your life—today, this moment, right now—to purposefully transform your "Uns" list from negative to positive? Whatever it is, reach for it now, embrace it! Don't place it on an empty shelf high up in the corner.

Reach for it now and use it.

---

## My Greatest Fear

As a general rule, I try to give worry and fear as little room in my life as possible. Several years ago, I made the conscious decision not to fall prey to worry and fear, because both are a waste of my imagination, my mental energy, and a very real threat to my sense of inner tranquility and balance. Both are joy-stealers . . . and both can become extremely rude and greedy if they are allowed to become so.

Still, you'll notice that I didn't say I *never* worry. I didn't say I'm *never* fearful. As I've mentioned in previous chapters, *never* is a word I, well, never use—or at the very least, I try my best to studiously avoid, if only because I am human, and human nature is beautifully fluid. In my world, *never* and *always* rarely exist. I hold a multitude within me—countless layers, ways, and dimensions of doing, being, leading, and living. *Never* and *always* slam the door on my ability to be fully human.

That said, though, I do hold onto *one* fear—but it's important to note that I hold onto this fear with a sense of purpose and intention. I hold onto this fear because it drives me, it propels me forward, and it helps define the work that I do as a leader, a motivator, an executive, a change agent, and as a human being who is deeply committed to helping others become the most authentic version of themselves that they can possibly be:

My greatest fear is *unrecognized potential.*

Whether it is seeing unrecognized potential in myself, in my colleagues or employees, in the members of my own family, or even in people I don't even know, it doesn't just break my heart—it *moves me to action*!

So I count this particular fear as a blessing of sorts, because it lights a continual fire within me to help others move from stuck to unstoppable in their own lives. This is my life's work. This is why I have devoted such time and energy into developing these stuck-to-unstoppable principles. I offer them as way to remind people that when they actually apply these principles on a consistent basis, they will be able to develop—and here I'll use those two, beautiful words I used at the beginning of this chapter—*actionable strategies* to move towards growth, towards positive change, and towards the miracle of renewed momentum.

The beauty of unrecognized potential—and yes, there is an element of beauty in unrecognized potential—is its transformative ability to shift into something else entirely. That we, as humans, can make the conscious decision to move from being the victim to becoming the victor—from choosing faith over fear and action over inaction—is a blessing of untold magnitude. What does it take to generate this momentum? First and foremost, it takes awareness, which is precisely where we began.

> Ask yourself, as you begin your own journey towards being consistently unstoppable: Am I doing all that I can—everything that I can—to help those around me recognize their potential in the fullest sense of the word?

If the answer that comes back is, "No, I'm not really doing everything that I can do help others recognize their full potential," don't beat yourself up about it. If anything, be grateful that you asked yourself the honest question and received the honest answer, because it tells you that as a leader and a human, you've got work to do. We all do. You are not alone.

The beauty of it all, though, is that we can use this Stuck-to-Unstoppable Playbook together now. We do it individually, of course—as these principles relate to and fit comfortably into the contours of our own lives—but collectively as well, to help create a greater good in the world around us. Such a thing is possible: we can customize these plays, but we can also weave together a commonly held set of beliefs, values, and principles that can be enjoyed, felt, and shared by us all. It is up to us to make this happen.

Another effective way to address this fear—perhaps you share it too, this fear of unrecognized potential in yourself and/or in others—is to ask yourself a few reflective questions. These must be deeply probative, brutally honest questions that might even make you feel a bit uncomfortable because they will take you to a place of raw truth and deep-down inner reflection—but we know, now, that this "inner place" is where growth lives and breathes.

Ask yourself a series of questions that allow you to truly evaluate and reflect upon your ability and/or inability to push past stuck. Turn inward and ask: *What is prohibiting me from taking action towards getting unstuck? I know I am stuck, but what is moving within me that is preventing me from taking forward-moving action? Why do these things hold such power over me? How can I change my relationship to these forces that keep me bound in this uncomfortable space?*

Asking yourself these kinds of introspective, soul-searching questions should be helpful in directing you to the next thing you'll need: action. As a possible course of action, then, consider making a list of these impediments and obstacles you've just identified. Write them down. Visualize them. Make them real. Take the purposeful step of sorting them into buckets. *Then throw away any that are not actionable.*

Keep this list reasonable and realistic. If there are things on your list that cannot be changed because they are out of your control, then let them go. *Let them go!* As soon as you do, you will probably feel a sense of sweet surrender and a greater sense of ownership and accountability. Identify the things you can control and toss the things you cannot control overboard. Cast them off the side of your ship. Let them sink into the deep, deep water. You do not need them anymore.

From the items that remain on your list, select the low-hanging fruit first! By this, I mean focus on a few of the things that can be changed without an extraordinary amount of effort—the easy wins that will add wind to your sails and momentum to your journey. Then move to the larger challenges that will require more time, more resources, and more energy.

Most important, remain focused and consistent. Start will small steps . . . but keep on stepping. Do not stop. Before you know it, the small steps will turn into larger steps, and the larger steps will lead you onto an entirely new path—a path of your own making. Baby steps are good. Cherish the baby steps.

As you continue on your journey, I need to emphasize again that you are not walking alone. You are not sailing alone. There are others at your side. Others just behind you, others still ahead of you, and still others whose masts have not yet even appeared on the horizon . . . but they are coming. They are on their way. Everywhere you look, the sea will be filled with the bright, beautiful masts of other ships. We make up a multitude.

---

## The Invitation

That we do make up a multitude, and that we do possess the shining awareness that we are on this journey together is yet another vital concept that I have tried to emphasize throughout this book. Now that we have entered every room of our literary home, we have come closer to making this home feel like it is our own.

Now you can decorate it however you like. Rearrange the furniture! Toss in some colorful throw pillows! You can even add on a spare room or repurpose one of those cluttered closets. The point is that this home belongs to *you* now. You are the architect. But equally important, we have traveled though these rooms together. The journey is not just yours . . . it is ours.

And although our literary journey has come to an end, our collective journey towards becoming consistently unstoppable is only just beginning. Let that be a comfort to you: you are now, in some way, aligned with the other leaders and readers who have come along on this literary journey. There is a common bond between us, a dialogue that has been initiated, and a shared kinship that has been established.

I, for one, do not want to lose this bond. If anything, I want to issue the invitation to you that we strengthen this bond of common purpose and shared understanding that has grown as a result of our "house tour." The way we experience continued growth (at least one way that I have discovered and deeply cherish) is through shared experience and the continuous exchange of wisdom and enlightenment.

Why must our journey end simply because the *book* ends? If you'd like to share some of the stuck-to-unstoppable experiences you encounter moving forward and keep the conversation going, I invite you to connect with me on social media.

The path is before you—miles of open road. Will there be bumps and detours along the way? You bet there will be. But learn to cherish those bumps, because *now* you hold the road-map that will guide you around and over them.

The path ahead belongs to you.

Which direction you take, at which speed, and with whom, is entirely up to you.

Always remember this most beautiful fact—and this time, I use the word *always* with intention and purpose: the gift of conscious choice lies within you.

Always.

# Acknowledgments

THIS SECTION OF THE BOOK reminds me of a time when I received an annual bonus based on my performance at work.

I was a single mom. My older kids, Howie and Samantha, were in college, so it was just my youngest son, Dylan, and I at home.

We went out to lunch to celebrate, and I presented *him* with a "bonus" check. When he asked me what it was for, I explained to him that if not for his cool, low-maintenance style and maturity far beyond his years—he was the tender age of nine at the time—I would not have been able to earn this extra money. We talked about how his behavior directly correlated to my effectiveness at work and our overall success as a family. He got it then, and he continues to get it. I share this with you to emphasize that we rarely go it alone.

On that note, my heartfelt thanks to the following people, experiences, and memories that have been instrumental in the creation of this book.

Every once in a while, particularly when you detach from what you are most longing for, it suddenly gets dumped right into your lap. It literally appears out of nowhere. I love when that happens because it restores my faith in the Universe. Other times, you get completely bamboozled! In walks Sully. All kidding aside, you are extraordinary. I am so deeply grateful for you and all of your support and encouragement throughout this process—thank you from the bottom of my heart!

To my editor, Kristin Clark Taylor for the magic you bring to every conversation, your warmth, your kind and humble spirit, and the copious amounts of laughter (and tears!). I am so grateful I get to call you my friend.

To my publishing family at Amplify and Mascot Books: CEO Naren Aryal for your enthusiastic belief in me and your gentle way of getting things done; project manager Brandon Coward for always answering my phone calls, shepherding me through this process, and pushing me to dig deeper, knowing what I was aiming to achieve; and the design and marketing teams, who helped make this book beautiful and visible. To my 3RC crew, especially Josh Linkner and Connor Trombley—I adore you both for a kazillion reasons.

To my stellar tribe of girls! From Olean to Niagara, Charlotte to Belleair, San Diego to LA and everywhere in between, you know who you are! You are the dearest of friends, and I remain so happy and grateful we continue to endure this sometimes-tortured path of life together.

Special thanks to my partner in crime, Laurie Karkoski. Who knew what would come out of that fateful introduction at Team Disney in 1996. I will just sit here and smile. There are no words, truly.

To Lee Cockerell, a mentor of thirty years and someone I am deeply grateful to also call a friend—you are a never-ending source of inspiration and positivity who has made an indelible mark on my life. You are a gift that I cherish immensely.

To my Dad—for your love and so many life lessons, especially for teaching me how to hunt and fish at a young age.

To Lynn—for always having my back. I am so lucky to have you in my life.

To my brothers, Bill and Tim—when one's buying, the other one's selling. So glad I get to be the beneficiary of all you each have to offer. You've been my lifeline.

Howie, Samantha, Dylan—thank you for hanging in there with me. We've been on quite the ride! My heart is full and deeply grateful for all of your inspiration, laughter, encouragement, love, and forgiveness. I am immensely proud of you.

To my mom, Donna Sweet, who taught me to lead with love. You were my first leader, my first hero. Thank you for teaching me the importance of courage, discipline, and consistency in life and leadership. You continue to amaze and inspire me every day!

# About the Author

**TRISH HUNT** is the president of a division of a S&P 500 drug and consumer health global manufacturing company. She is also the producer and host of the national television and radio show *The Hunt with Trish Hunt.*

With more than thirty years of progressive operational and leadership experience at both Fortune 500 and startup-stage companies in a range of industries, she has dedicated her life to helping individuals, teams, and organizations break out of ruts and achieve unstoppable momentum towards their goals.

She holds a master's degree in organizational change and leadership and a bachelor's in hospitality management. She recently added empty nester to her résumé, with two kids successfully launched into the real world while the youngest continues to joyfully make his way through college.